# WATERFALLS

## OF THE BLUE RIDGE

# WATERFALLS

## OF THE BLUE RIDGE

A Hiking Guide to the Cascades of the —
————Blue Ridge Mountains

**THIRD EDITION**

NICOLE BLOUIN
STEVE BORDONARO
MARILOU WIER BORDONARO

MENASHA RIDGE PRESS
BIRMINGHAM, ALABAMA

**For my grandfather, Jack M. Blouin.**
In this way, I can share something of my world—waterfalls and
the Blue Ridge Mountains.

*—Nicole*

**To Megan and Cory, our heart and soul.**
May your paths be long and happy and always lead to waterfalls.

*—Steve and Marilou*

Copyright © 1994, 1996, 2003 by Nicole Blouin, Steve Bordonaro,
and Marilou Wier Bordonaro. All Rights Reserved.
Printed in Canada. Third edition, first printing.
Published by Menasha Ridge Press. Distributed by Globe Pequot Press

Photos © Kevin Adams: Indian Creek, p. 21; Whitaok Canyon #1, p. 28; Whiteoak
Canyon #2, p. 29; St. Mary's, p. 38; Falling Spring, p. 55; Roaring Run, p. 57; Lower
Cascades, p. 64; Elk, p. 85; Catawba, p. 97; High Shoals, p. 103; Bridal Veil, p. 123;
Courthouse, p. 133; Toxaway, p. 146; Glen, p. 159; Little Creek, p. 166; Soco, p. 170;
Rufus Morgan, p. 183; and color-insert images of Elk, Big Laurel, Tom Branch, and
Falling Spring.

Photos © Nicole Blouin: Tory's Den, p. 66; Widow's Creek, p. 72; Roaring Fork, p.
90; Crabtree, p. 93; Douglas, p. 108; Graveyard Fields, p. 139; Rainbow, p. 152;
Lower Cullasaja, p. 161; and color-insert images of Lower Cascades, Whitewater,
Upper Catawba, Widow's Creek, Douglas, Cullasaja River, and Lower Cullasaja.

Photos © Ben Keys: Linville, p. 83; Raven Cliff, p. 126; and Mill Shoals, p. 132.

Cover and text design: Ian Szymkowiak (Palace Press International).

Cover photos: Cullasaja Gorge © Nicole Blouin and Linville Falls © Ben Keys.

Library of Congress Cataloging-in-Publication Data
Blouin, Nicole, 1966–
  Waterfalls of the Blue Ridge/Nicole Blouin, Steve Bordonaro, Marilou Wier
Bordonaro.–3rd ed.
  p. cm.
Includes bibliographical references and index.
ISBN 0-89732-551-6
  1. Hiking–Blue Ridge Parkway (N.C. and Va.)–Guidebooks. 2. Trails–Blue Ridge
Parkway (N.C. and Va.)–Guidebooks. 3. Waterfalls–Virginia–Guidebooks. 4. Water-
falls–North Carolina–Guidebooks. 5. Blue Ridge Parkway (N.C. and Va.)–Guide-
books. I. Bordonaro, Steve 1951– II. Bordonaro, Marilou Wier, 1950– III. Title.
GV199.42.B65B56 2003
917.5504'44–dc21                                             20003051434

Menasha Ridge Press
P.O. Box 43673
Birmingham, Alabama 35243
www.menasharidge.com

# CONTENTS

## Section Four APPENDICES AND INDEX

# LIST OF MAPS

# AcknowLedgments

I am happy that the publisher saw the need for a revision of this book and I would like to give credit to those who made the update possible. My role was primarily to tie together the contributions of the many people who were involved. Any merit from this new edition is due in part to those mentioned in the following.

I drew on the expertise of chambers of commerce, the park service, the forest service, and other agencies and organizations, as well as individuals who love waterfalls. Their cooperation immensely added to the revision of this work. I would like to highlight a few of these people. Thanks to:

Joanne Amberson with Shenandoah National Park.

Joan Leake with the Greater Augusta Regional Chamber of Commerce.

Lori Nealis with the Luray-Page Chamber of Commerce.

Kathy Hall with the Pedlar-Glenwood Ranger District.

Edward Farr with Stone Mountain State Park.

Howard Gray with the Blowing Rock Chamber of Commerce.

Peter Givens, Randy Sutton, Tina Charlebois, and Michele Maertans with the Parkway.

Anita Aaron with Natural Bridge of Virginia.

Jerry Jacobsen with the New Castle Ranger District.

Forrest Gladden with Douthat State Park.

Kim Woodson with the Alleghany Chamber of Commerce.

Dick Schaddelee with the Bryson City Chamber of Commerce.

Nancy Gray with Great Smoky Mountains National Park.

Chrissy Arch with the Cherokee Welcome Center.

Jaye Dow with Hanging Rock State Park.

Nancy Issac with the Avery County Chamber of Commerce.

Michael Rouse and Rod Birdsong with the McDowell Chamber of Commerce.

Peggy Hinckle with Mt. Mitchell State Park.

Marla Tambellini with the Asheville Chamber of Commerce.

Paul Bradley and Derek Ibarguen with the Toecane Ranger District.

Jeff Jennings with DuPont State Forest.

Steve Pagano with Gorges State Park.

South Mountains State Park.

Franklin Chamber of Commerce.

Chad Boniface with the Highlands Ranger District.

Mary at Chimney Rock Park.

Sally Browning with the Wayah Ranger District.

Sue Bumgarner with the Cashiers Chamber of Commerce.

Tim Lee and Joe Anderson at Caesar's Head State Park.

Beth Carden at the Brevard Chamber of Commerce.

Diane Bolt with the Pisgah Ranger District.

Greg Wilson, who attends Clemson University, for hiking to the new Franklin waterfalls.

*—Nicole Blouin*

A project of this magnitude required the assistance of people too numerous to mention. There are a few, however, whose help proved invaluable, and to whom we wish to express our appreciation.

Thanks to: Jim Bob and Dottie Tinsley for leading us to the waterfalls and inspiring us to "keep on trekking;" Skip Dunn for leading us to the Tinsleys; Jack Hall of the Lake Toxaway Company for his valuable input and his generous gift of time; Sue Elderkin and Don Dyer of the U.S. Forest Service, Pisgah District of the Pisgah National Forest, for their facts and directions; Patricia and Clark Grosvenor of the Key Falls Inn for their gracious hospitality and Beth Womble of the Womble Inn for hers; Esther Wesley of the Brevard Chamber of Commerce for her guidance; Tim and Peg Hansen of Highland Books in Brevard for their resources and assistance; and John Barbour of the Nantahala Outdoor Center for his input.

We would also like to thank our parents, Tommy and Marianne Wier, as well as Laura, Jerry, and Jennifer Jackson, for entertaining Megan and Cory those many weekends we were working on the book. And thanks to Megan and Cory, who have shared a lot of our explorations and who have displayed patience far beyond their years.

Finally, thanks to Nicole Blouin and Michael Jones for allowing us to be involved in this project. It opened our eyes to our own "backyard."

*—Steve and Marilou Bordonaro*

# THE BLUE RIDGE

PA
PHILADELPHIA
NJ
OH
MD
Front Royal
DE
Skyline Drive →
WASHINGTON D.C.
64
WV
RICHMOND
KY
← Blue Ridge Parkway
64
ROANOKE
VA
TN
Cherokee
RALEIGH
NC
85
SC
ATLANTA
95
GA
Atlantic Ocean

## MAPS LEGEND

 **LOWER CASCADES**

*Waterfall Parking and Trailhead*

**LURAY**

*Base Town*

**ROANOKE**

*City*

**RICHMOND**

*Capital City*

*Appalachian Trail*

◆

*Blue Ridge Parkway or Skyline Drive*

*Point of Interest*

**63**

*Interstate Highways*

*U.S. Highways*

*State Highways*

**VIRGINIA**

*State Boundary*

**Lake Blue**

**Blue River**

*Lake or River*

 *Visitors Center*

*Point of Interest*

 **Mt. Maggie 3312'**

*Mountain with Height in Feet*

*Compass Rose*

# INTRODUCTION

Waterfalls are perhaps nature's most captivating wonder. They are magical, holding all the secrets of the woods. Although they seem simple—falling water—we are astonished at finding one of these moving spectacles hidden within the folds of the forest.

Mountain streams leave their birthplace, stretching and rushing towards the sea. They are fed by springs and rains as they travel down ancient slopes following channels carved out centuries before. Reaching a precipice, they fall, creating an enchanting place to become lost in time and space.

For some people, waterfalls are simply excellent places to picnic. For others, waterfalls are the center of all wild places. Whichever the case, waterfalls make you feel good. Their therapeutic powers are similar to the cozy glow of a toasty fire, the endless rolling of the ocean surf, or a drumming rainstorm. Some scientists believe this is because of the negative ions they produce.

Remember when you were a kid and you'd plan your attack on an Oreo® cookie? You'd twist the chocolate wafer apart and dig your teeth into the filling until the cream surface resembled tire tracks in the snow. The chocolate wafers were nice, but the cream filling was a special treat. The same can be said about walking in the woods and discovering a waterfall. A hike could stand alone, but it is even better when combined with the chance to visit a waterfall.

Waterfall hiking in the mountains of the Blue Ridge is a marvelous way to experience the outdoors. Trails to waterfalls lead through national forests and parks, through state and city parks, and even through private and commercial properties.

You can seek out a different waterfall every time or hike to a favorite falls over and over. During an early morning walk, you might catch a glimpse of a wild animal drinking from a pool below the falls. Or you could camp beside a waterfall and fall asleep to the sound of rushing water.

Having seen one waterfall, you have not seen them all. Falls are all different, taking on many shapes and forms. A waterfall might drop off a sheer cliff or cascade down a slide. A waterfall might flow over several drops in a row, or plunge into a pool and then cascade again further downstream.

Waterfalls often have interesting names, sometimes more mysterious than telling. Silver Run Falls has a beautiful name; Blue Suck Falls has an unusual name. Like many waterfalls, Soco Falls and Lower Cullasaja Falls get their names from Indian words. Carter Creek Falls is also called Douglas Falls. Others share common names, such as Upper Falls or Cascades. When setting off to a waterfall, keep in mind that there may be another with the same name elsewhere and the falls may be known locally by a different name, or none at all—simply as "the waterfall."

Each waterfall has its own personality. Some are exceptional for the water volume they command, others for the tremendous height from which they fall. The personality of a waterfall changes with each rainfall. Rain saturates the ground and fuels the creeks and rivers. Falls swell with an abundance of water—a delicate cascade might be a raging waterfall on the next visit, and vice versa. Thus, waterfalls invite visitors to return again and again.

The personality of a waterfall changes with the seasons. The colors reflected in a clear mountain stream shift from pastels and greens to shades of autumn and earth tones. As the months progress, foliage around the falls blooms, flourishes, and withers away. One month, a flower grows out of a crack in the rock, watered by the constant spray of the falls; another, an icicle hangs overhead.

Visit a waterfall in the spring and you'll see a pink-and-purple procession of flowering mountain laurel and rhododendron. Waterfalls overflow from April rains, which bring May wildflowers to blanket the earth. The hillsides cry out for a wedding.

In the summer, you'll enjoy the cool mist that drifts lazily off the face of the falls. This time of year, you can allow the waterfall to absorb you. Sink into the swimming hole at the base of the falls, lean back, and let the water cascade over you.

Visit a waterfall in autumn to be surrounded by the brilliant reds, yellows, and oranges of the hardwood forest. Color frames the white frothy cascade; painted leaves swirl and dance on the surface of the clear stream. Lie on a warm rock and bask in the sun for awhile. The days of Indian summer, with crisp air and cloudless skies, beckon woodland adventurers.

Subdued by winter, the wilderness offers wonderful solitude. Waterfalls ice to create picturesque sculptures dangling from rocky cliffs. Snow blankets the forest floor, and bare trees provide unobstructed views.

The hills of the Blue Ridge harbor an incredible number of waterfalls. Visitors, and even locals, are usually unaware of how many extraordinary cascades adorn the area. The waterfall "collector" will find heaven in the Blue Ridge, where hundreds of "named" waterfalls, and perhaps thousands more, are waiting to be discovered any time of year.

Grand or gorgeous or graceful, bubbling brook or roaring river, we've never met a waterfall we didn't like.

*Welcome to the waterfalls of the Blue Ridge!*

# THE BASICS OF BLUE RIDGE

## WATERFALLS

SECTION *one*

# about THIS GUIDE

**T**HIS BOOK IS A COLLECTION of more than 100 waterfalls in the Blue Ridge Mountains. The waterfalls range in height from 10 feet to 500 feet. Some require no hike at all, while others can only be seen from the trail, with hikes of up to 10-miles round trip. For the purpose of this book, we roughly defined the Blue Ridge as the mountainous region along the Blue Ridge Parkway between Great Smoky Mountains National Park and Shenandoah National Park.

*Waterfalls of the Blue Ridge* will take you to two states, Virginia and North Carolina (with an optional junket over the border to South Carolina); four national forests, George Washington, Jefferson, Pisgah, and Nantahala; three national parks, Shenandoah, Blue Ridge Parkway, and Great Smoky Mountains; seven state parks, Douthat, Hanging Rock, Stone Mountain, Mount Mitchell, South Mountains, Gorges, and Ceasar's Head; three wilderness areas, St. Mary's, Linville Gorge, and Southern Nantahala; two private parks, Natural Bridge of Virginia and Chimney Rock; a state forest, DuPont; and the Cherokee Indian Reservation. Add to that list a city park, a trip by boat on a lake, and several tracts of private land.

The waterfalls are grouped together according to their proximity to a particular town (we call these base towns ) or their location in a state park. Each chapter describes a different base town or state park in Virginia or North Carolina, followed by details on several waterfalls with directions. The waterfalls appear in roughly geographic order, north to south.

To arrange a day of waterfall hiking, look under the chapter for the base town or state park you plan to visit. Using the maps and information provided, you can plan hikes that fit your time limitations and physical ability. Choose a waterfall trail on which to can spend the whole afternoon or chart out a circuit and visit several in one day, as you prefer. We've provided trail distances and difficulty, waterfall descriptions, and general directions.

## TRAIL DISTANCE

The mileage listed for each hike is recorded as the total distance—round trip (there and back along the same footpath or on a loop). A pedometer, a simple instrument that hooks to your waist and calculates mileage by stride length, was used when accurate trail length was not posted or otherwise available. All mileage is specified to the nearest tenth.

If you are not good at judging distance, we suggest that you purchase a pedometer. This gadget will prove useful when someone asks, "How much farther is it?" The pedometer can be fairly reliable if used correctly.

To estimate how long it will take you to hike a certain distance, take into account your hiking style, your physical condition, and the trail conditions. The average hiker covers about 2 miles per hour.

## TRAIL DIFFICULTY

The ratings for trail difficulty are based on the amount of energy expended by an average, healthy person. More effort is needed for each level—easy, moderate, and strenuous. Trail difficulty generally reflects elevation gained per mile. The longer and steeper the grade, the more difficult the trail.

**Easy** It is possible to hike an easy trail without getting tired. The gradient is generally flat with slight inclines.

**Moderate** You may be somewhat winded and need an occasional rest on a moderate hike. The trail will have some modest inclines.

**Strenuous** The average hiker will definitely feel the workout on a strenuous trail. Several breaks may be necessary. The trail will have steep sections.

## WATERFALL DESCRIPTIONS

Waterfalls are often described using a stack of superlatives: the highest, the widest, and the most beautiful. Such descriptions often neglect details and overlook the character of a waterfall. We tried to be informative by using specific details. Each waterfall description gives an estimated height of the falls and other details like width, number of tiers, average flow, and angle of the falling water. We tried to find the story behind the falls whenever possible.

Most people prefer a waterfall with lots of volume, but the beauty of a waterfall is not necessarily tied to its rate of flow. Some waterfalls are always powerful, while others fluctuate dramatically with rainfall. If you want to see a waterfall at its most forceful, visit in the spring. Or, watch the weather. Sometimes, it just takes one good thunderstorm.

## DIRECTIONS

The most frustrating aspect of researching this book was getting lost. We got so lost, so many times! One intention of this guide is to spare you, the reader, similar travails. It would take pages to describe every mile of road and every foot of trail, but we did our best to make our directions as clear as possible to help you stay found.

Detailed driving directions, positioned at the end of each waterfall entry, will get you to the trailhead. The location of a trailhead is always indicated. Maps at the beginning of each chapter help you identify the falls relative to one another and the surrounding towns and roads. However, they are not intended to replace the driving directions. General trail information, positioned within the waterfall entry, will get you to the waterfall.

On the road, be aware that street signs change and new roads alter routes. On the trail, don't rely completely on blazes or markers, which are susceptible to vandalism. On private land, keep in mind that a landowner who allowed access in the past may choose not to let you onto the property. No trespassing signs must be respected.

To find out more about a waterfall, a trail, or an area, go to the back of the book. The appendix lists an address and phone number for every chapter, either a local chamber of commerce or a state park headquarters. It also includes contact information for Shenandoah National Park, Great Smoky Mountains National Park, and the Blue Ridge Parkway.

## WILDERNESS ETHICS AND ETIQUETTE

More and more hikers visit the mountains of the Blue Ridge every year. Waterfall trails are especially popular destinations. The problems of overuse are evident: soil erosion, overcrowding, litter, and decreasing numbers of wildlife and vegetation. Wild places are for solitude and splendor. Those who love wild places can help preserve them.

In addition to the following list, we encourage you to consider doing two things. First, adopting one waterfall trail, officially or unofficially, that you can hike at least four times a year. Volunteer with the park headquarters, when applicable, to perform trail maintenance. And second, on your waterfall hikes, carry a trash bag and spend a few minutes picking up after someone less courteous. A little effort makes a tangible difference.

**Stay on maintained trails.** Safeguard against crushing sensitive plants and increasing soil erosion by not straying from designated paths. Trail builders strive to create a path that has good erosion control and as little impact on vegetation as possible. Do not walk off the trail, even to avoid muddy stretches, because this destroys the border and enlarges the trail. Switchbacks are the most often abused trail sections. Avoiding the temptation to take a shortcut can save future scars on the hillside.

**Travel quietly in the woods.** You are less likely to intrude upon other hikers, as well as the wildlife, when you walk and talk quietly. When taking a break, be courteous of those passing by. Don't block the trail or block someone's view of the falls with your picnic

**Hike during the off-season.** Help spread out visitor use by taking advantage of the off-season. Off-season doesn't necessarily mean winter. Try going on weekdays or very early in the morning.

**Travel in small groups.** You lessen your impact on the trail and on other visitors when you're not hiking with a crowd. Large groups (ten people or more) cause a disproportionate invasion of narrow trails and small overlooks.

**Pack everything out.** You can contribute to the beauty of the woods by not adding anything. This principle includes biodegradable material; food scraps are unsightly and attract pests. If you bury leftovers, animals may dig them up. Plan ahead—reduce the amount you pack in and carry a bag specifically for packing out waste.

**Respect wildlife.** When you enter the wilderness, you are traveling in other creatures' homes. Try to minimize your impact on wildlife. It is particularly important not to feed wild animals, for your safety and theirs.

**Leave the things of nature in their place.** You afford others the opportunity to enjoy the same experience that you enjoyed if you do not disturb the natural environment. If every hiker dug up a flower or collected an edible plant, we would quickly deplete an area. Take a photograph of the fire pink and only an occasional sample from the blackberry bush, and you will help protect the vegetation of our backcountry.

## WARNINGS AND WATERFALL SAFETY

Oh no! More rules? That's what we thought. But after talking with rangers, park employees, and city officials throughout the Blue Ridge, we discovered that accidents around waterfalls are a serious problem. Don't climb on slippery rocks or atop a falls. Lovely waterfalls often hide lethal danger. Crabtree Falls (Virginia) has claimed 23 lives to date.

Developed areas can be just as dangerous as undeveloped areas. As one ranger put it, "It is just the nature of rocks and water and cliffs. You can build observation decks and post signs, but people will be careless and use poor judgment."

The hazards are real. So, instead of incorporating "a single slip could be your last" into every chapter, we decided to outline the basics of waterfall safety here. Please, be careful.

» Stay on developed trails and don't stray from observation points or platforms.

» Watch your footing. Rocks may be slippery, and algae-coated areas are unforgiving.

» The top of any waterfall is, of course, the most dangerous part. Avoid the temptation to lean over a ledge at the top of the falls.

» Exercise caution on the trail to the falls, as well as around the falls themselves. Waterfall trails are often treacherous—steep and rocky with sheer embankments.

» Be especially cautious when taking photographs. You are likely to pay more attention to your camera than to your footing.

» Watch children carefully. Children should always be under the immediate supervision of an adult.

» And watch your dog. Our golden retriever, who was surefooted but didn't understand the concept of slick rocks, fell off a 12-foot drop. He was fine, but we were nearly injured scurrying down to him.

» Never hike alone.

On any hike, carry a small day pack or fanny pack with useful items and extra gear. Most people consider ten items essential: matches, a compass, a map, a knife, a flashlight, sunglasses, fire kindling, extra food, extra clothing, and a first-aid kit. Add Ziploc® bags to the list for waterproofing and organizing. And be sure to carry an adequate supply of water. Don't drink any surface water unless it has been boiled for one minute or treated with chemicals.

The proceeding list may seem long, but the first six essentials can fit into one Ziploc® bag. Extra food and clothing (a few candy bars and a raincoat or sweater) don't take up much space. Avid hikers sometimes keep a day pack filled and ready to go, checking the contents occasionally, testing batteries, restocking first-aid supplies, and adding to food reserves as necessary.

## PHOTOGRAPHING WATERFALLS

We try to photograph every waterfall we visit, preserving the collection in a scrapbook. These aren't all quality photographs—just snapshots to preserve a memory. Most of the photographs that we take of waterfalls aren't great. We've spent a lot of time shooting waterfalls, but getting an excellent waterfall shot takes time, effort, and luck.

For the best effect, you need a tripod, slow film, and early morning or late afternoon light. Capturing the personality of a waterfall may mean several visits during different times of the year. The photographs in this book are not from our snapshot waterfall album. They are the result of years of hard work, early morning wake-up calls, shooting and reshooting, and lots and lots of film.

In the process, we gained some solid insight that relates directly to waterfall photography. We had the good fortune of doing a half dozen waterfall hikes with a professional photographer. On each, we watched her work and discovered something new. We also read several outdoor photography books and magazines that revealed tips about shooting moving water. Here is a summary of the basics. (If you are using a digital camera, most, but not all, considerations apply.)

**Tripod.** You'll need a sturdy tripod because you can't hold a camera sufficiently steady when using slow shutter speeds. Be sure the tripod is compact and lightweight so you'll be willing to carry it with you no matter how long the hike. Use a cable release, a cord attached to the shutter button that separates you from the camera. This reduces shake caused by pressing the shutter button. A good minimum length for a cable release is 12 inches, and buy a spare because they are easily misplaced. Our tripod rule: Use a tripod whenever you can, especially if the shutter speed is less than the lens focal length. For example, don't handhold a 50 mm lens when using a shutter speed slower than 1/60 of a second.

**Film Speed.** You need slow film to use slow shutter speeds. Generally, an ISO rating between 25 and 100 is suggested for scenics, although ISO 100 is somewhat fast for waterfalls. These slow films have a fine grain and produce the sharpest images. To see every detail, use the slowest film possible for each particular lighting condition.

**Shutter Speed.** Slow shutter speeds give a sense of movement. Mike Wyatt, in his book *Basic Essentials of Photography Outdoors,* explains how shutter speed relates to moving current. "The movement of flowing water will be completely stopped at 1/2000 second. The fastest portions of the water will begin to soften at 1/60 second. At 1/15 second, the water's movement will be clearly evident, but the water will not be completely blurred." Most waterfall photographs are shot at 1/8 second or slower to produce a soft quality.

**Time of Day.** Midday sun creates harsh lighting and shadows. Visit a waterfall at daybreak or an hour before sunset, and observe the wonderful quality of the light. The light is softer, colors are richer.

**Exposure.** The white water of a falls will often cause your light meter to underexpose your shot, making the water gray and the foliage slightly dark. You can open up the lens a little and cross your fingers, or you can bracket. Bracketing means shooting images at the original reading and at increments in each direction (usually half stop increments). If you shoot one on, two over, and two under, you should get what you want.

**Perspective.** Waterfall photographs need a reference to indicate their size. To give a feeling of depth and space, use foreground elements, such as trees, rocks, and people. In essence, try to frame the waterfall.

**Position.** Shoot from the top, bottom, or side of the falls, but always try to keep one side of the image frame parallel to the ground. Basically, treat the waterfall like a piece of architecture.

**People.** The high reflectance of water makes your meter tend to underexpose people in a waterfall photograph. Open up one to two stops, meter off a gray card or set the exposure by reading only the subject.

**Rainbows.** If you are lucky enough to find a rainbow at the end of a waterfall, burn a lot of film. Don't miss the opportunity for a spectacular photograph by skimping on film. Underexpose slightly to increase the color saturation–bracket one to two stops.

**Other Notes.** Watch the sun because light reflecting in the lens between the glass surfaces can cause a flare (diffused spot) or a ghost (multi-sided bright spot). Look for the sun in the periphery. Horizon because horizon lines should be level, and in general, not placed in the center of the composition. Blah skies have no place in a great photo. If the sky isn't deep blue, contrasted by white clouds, or intensely colorful, compose your shot without it. In the image area, look for wasted space, light and dark areas, and distracting elements. Before you press the shutter button (or cable release), follow the rectangle of the viewing screen with your eyes.

## about THE BLUE RIDGE

### THE BLUE RIDGE MOUNTAINS

Join us on an adventure through the Blue Ridge Mountains. Our fascination with waterfalls brought us here. In our search, we discovered a region rich in natural and human history and encountered physical beauty so compelling that it defies description. It is said that to share a joy is to multiply it. We would like to share the joy of our discoveries with you.

The Blue Ridge Mountains run from southeastern Pennsylvania to northwestern Georgia. They form the eastern portion of the Appalachian Mountains, the great range that extends 1,600 miles from Quebec Province to Alabama. In Virginia, the Blue Ridge Mountains divide the Piedmont from the Shenandoah Valley. In North Carolina, they form the eastern section of a mountain chain that is more than 75 miles wide and includes the Black Mountains and the Great Smokies.

When seen from a distance, the forested slopes of the Blue Ridge project their bluish tone because of water droplets and gas molecules released into the air by the trees. William Byrd of Virginia was one of the first to note this ever-present blue color in 1728 when he surveyed the boundary between Virginia and North Carolina. Byrd described the distant horizon as "ranges of blue clouds rising one above another." Sadly, however, research is showing that these views are changing at an alarming rate due to the rapidly increasing haze of man-made pollution.

### STORY OF THE MOUNTAINS

The story of the formation of the Blue Ridge Mountains is not a simple one. These mountains are believed to be among the oldest in the world. Knowing something of their complicated history helps explain why the mountains exist in their present form. According to the concept of geologic change known as plate tectonics, the earth's crust is made up of gigantic, rigid plates of rock that are floating on the hot liquid mantle below. These crusts are always moving–grinding against one another, fusing together, and then breaking apart again.

The process that formed the Appalachians and the Blue Ridge began more than a billion years ago. Miles beneath the surface of the earth, molten magma slowly solidified into the core of what we now know as the Blue Ridge Mountains. Over millions of years, this basement rock folded and uplifted, collided with other land masses, lay under giant shallow seas, eroded, and once again thrust upward.

The last significant event probably occurred 200 million years ago when eastern North America collided with a continental fragment that was to become Africa. This collision caused the sea floor to fold, lift, and break apart. The older underlying layer of rock tilted upward and slid over the younger layer, creating the Appalachians. The continents fused for a period of perhaps 50 million years and then split again, the Atlantic Ocean filling the void between the separating land masses.

So, the mountains were formed, but there is more to the story. The rolling mountains we see today were once as jagged and craggy as the Himalayas. The rounded peaks of the Blue Ridge are largely a product of mechanical and chemical erosion. These forces have sculpted the mountains into peaceful swells shrouded with blue mist. Wind, water, and gravity continue to etch the face of the landscape inch by inch.

## HUMAN HISTORY

The history of the people who have lived in these mountains for centuries is as interesting as the story of the mountains' formation. Archaeological research has shown traces of human habitation in this area as early as 8,000 B.C. Evidence found at various sites throughout the mountains indicates that people have been in the Blue Ridge continuously since that time. American Indian tribes lived off this land before the arrival of Europeans. The first white men were hunters and traders in search of pelts. Many pioneers were kept away by tales of savages and other horrors. At the same time, the native Indians were being exterminated by other Indian raiders, as well as the whiskey and smallpox brought by fur traders and pioneers.

The colonists who came here were hardy stock. They were Scotch-Irish immigrants who had survived hard times in Northern Ireland, and Germans who came to escape the horrible conditions of the Thirty Years' War. They were joined by Englishmen from the coastal regions.

Before the American Revolution, many rebellious colonists entrenched themselves in the mountains. From their mountain strongholds, they fought and defeated the King's men during the Revolution. Later, the Cherokee were their foe. Eventually, the area came entirely under white control.

Because of their physical isolation, these Appalachian pioneers became self-sufficient. Schooling was rare. While many of the original settlers could read and write, often these skills gradually slipped away. Religion was the major influence in their lives. Traveling ministers carried the gospel to the isolated areas and were often the only outsiders. An old mountain saying, "Thar's nothing about in this weather but crows and Methodist ministers," hints at the ever-present influence of religion on a people shut off from outside civilization.

Roads were barely passable, when they existed at all. In waves, miners and loggers, enticed by rich ore veins and lush forests, depleted resources and departed. The mountain folk were left as destitute as before, and their land was desecrated.

The coming of the automobile, coupled with the increase in road building, brought change to the highlands. Electricity and modern conveniences made life somewhat easier for the mountaineers, but they maintained their self-sufficiency and their unique customs.

With the Blue Ridge Parkway came an interest in the lives of the colorful people who occupy the mountains and valleys of the Blue Ridge. Part of the stated purpose of the Blue Ridge Parkway is to preserve the history and culture of the highlanders.

## PLANTS AND ANIMALS

Just as we are intrigued by the history of the mountains and their inhabitants, we are captivated by the diversity of their natural wonders. There is no more ecologically complex woodland area in North America. Thousands of species have developed here over millions of years of evolution. The dramatic upheavals and shifting that formed the mountains also contributed to the great variety of plant life. Forerunners of rare botanical specimens were deposited in coves created by ancient glaciers.

The abundant rainfall, the mild climate, and the great variations in elevation make the Blue Ridge a paradise for botanists. Driving from the foothills of the Blue Ridge to the higher elevations, you encounter the same plant life zones that you would find driving from Georgia to Canada. Trees vary from the sycamore and river birch typical of Southeastern stream bottoms to spruce and fir forests similar to those found in northern Maine.

Naturalists also find the animal life of the region diverse and plentiful. Hikers frequently sight ground hogs, known as whistle pigs. There are also beaver, deer, bear, elk, foxes, opossums, chipmunks, squirrels, and skunks. Bird watchers in the Blue Ridge have a great opportunity because a major migratory flyway follows the mountains.

The Blue Ridge Mountains offer incredible seasonal variety. Spring and summer engage visitors with their constant palette of colors from brilliant to pastel, showcased against a tapestry of greens. Wildflowers, laurel, rhododendron, and flame azalea provide a procession of color that gives way to the spectacular blaze of fall. The muted tones of winter often belie the unpredictability of this season. The rime ice that adorns trees and rocks warns of the chill but provides a magnificent, sparkling picture. The clear, unobstructed panoramas in winter are beyond compare.

## THE BLUE RIDGE PARKWAY

The Blue Ridge Parkway forms the backbone of this marvelous scenic region. From Shenandoah National Park in Virginia to the Great Smoky Mountains National Park in North Carolina, it provides a platform from which to survey many of the wonders of the entire area. Writing in 1969 in *The Blue Ridge Parkway,* Harley E. Jolley describes it as "a road of unlimited horizons, a grand balcony."

The Parkway is also a masterful feat of engineering that has preserved the natural beauty and the cultural heritage of the Southern Highlands. Few of the millions of tourists who travel the scenic road each year have any concept of the hard labor, politics, and dreams that were involved in making the Parkway a reality. Considering the countless hardships and adversities, it is astonishing that the first rural national parkway in the United States was ever completed.

The Blue Ridge Parkway was designed as a Depression-era project to provide desperately needed jobs for the engineers, architects, and landscape architects, as well as the laborers of the Southern Highlands. The Park Service archives don't recognize a single originator of the idea. However, several people have taken credit. As early as 1909, Colonel Joseph Hyde Pratt, head of the North Carolina Geological Survey, dreamed of a scenic highway through the Blue Ridge Mountains. He even had a short section built before World War I diverted funds and manpower away from the project.

Several historians give credit for the Parkway to Virginia's Senator Harry F. Byrd. On an August day in 1933, Byrd was with President Franklin D. Roosevelt, who was on an inspection tour of the Civilian Conservation Corp (CCC) in the Shenandoah National Park. Roosevelt was very impressed with the Shenandoah's Skyline Drive (see Shenandoah National Park below). Byrd suggested the grandiose scheme of constructing a road connecting the Shenandoah National Park and the Great Smoky Mountains National Park. Roosevelt was enthusiastic and the wheels were set in motion. Secretary of the Interior Harold L. Ickes was asked to determine the route.

The problems confronting the Parkway were just beginning, and the project faced incredible obstacles, including debate over the actual path the road would take. Original plans directed the Parkway through North Carolina, Tennessee, and Virginia. Bitter fights between politicians from Tennessee and North Carolina placed Secretary Ickes in a difficult position. Amidst great protest from Tennessee officials, he opted for the so-called North Carolina route, stating that he found it to be more scenic and that the Pisgah and Nantahala National Forest would provide a good corridor for the scenic road.

There were many problems obtaining right-of-way, especially through the Cherokee Indian Reservation, which is the final link to the Great Smoky Mountains National Park. After years of negotiations between Cherokee and government officials, the Parkway was routed through the Cherokee Indian Reservation for many of its final miles.

The first rocks of the Parkway were blasted near Cumberland Knob, North Carolina, on September 11, 1935, but it was 52 years before the last 7.5 miles across Grandfather Mountain were completed. The landowners were intensely opposed to the route, and the final right-of-way was not granted until October 22, 1968. This missing link included the Linn Cove Viaduct, said to be one of the most intricate, segmented, concrete bridges ever constructed. This engineering marvel, which carries vehicles 1,240 feet across the face of Grandfather Mountain, ended the 14-mile detour on US 221. The final section of the Blue Ridge Parkway was completed and dedicated on September 11, 1987.

The Parkway begins at milepost 0 at Rockfish Gap, Virginia, the southern entrance to the Shenandoah National Park. For 469 miles, this scenic roadway closely follows the highest ridges of the Southern Appalachians. It ends at milepost 469.1, the entrance to the Great Smoky Mountains National Park and the land of the Cherokee. Along the way, the Parkway reaches elevations of over 6,000 feet, with an average 3,500 feet. For the first 355 miles, the Parkway closely follows the Blue Ridge in a southwesterly direction. For the remaining 114 miles, it follows the southern end of the imposing Black Mountains and threads through the Craggies, the Pisgahs, and the Balsams.

Traveling the Parkway, visitors are treated to a multitude of panoramic views, varying from dense forests to mile-high mountains. There are plateaus and farmland valleys where early settlers lived. Meadows are lined with split-rail fences and lush with wildflowers. You will see historic structures like old farm buildings and homesteads. The cultural sites and the sheer physical beauty preserved here make for a journey rich in history and inspiring scenery.

The one thing that you will not see on your journey is commercial development, although it is rapidly encroaching, especially around Roanoke and

Asheville. As a parkway, this road is designed and administered like any other national park, complete with overlooks, exhibits, displays, and interpretive signs. Park rangers work closely with naturalists, agronomists, and environmentalists to protect and restore what lies within the Parkway's domain.

Geographically located within one day's drive of one-half of the nation's population, the Blue Ridge Parkway is not meant to be a road to somewhere. It is a destination in itself. Millions of visitors come here for the camping facilities, trout-laden streams, picnic grounds, horseback riding, cross-country skiing, hiking trails, and of course, the waterfalls. The Blue Ridge Parkway will lead you to several waterfalls with easy-to-access trailheads at the parking areas and to overlooks directly alongside the road. Watch for the mileposts and enjoy the scenery along this famous drive.

## Friends of the Blue Ridge Parkway

The Blue Ridge Parkway is in danger—government funding doesn't cover the costs of all facilities and programs, and urban sprawl threatens the natural environment. Friends of the Blue Ridge Parkway is a nonprofit, volunteer organization dedicated to America's favorite scenic drive.

Through a variety of programs, its members strive to protect and preserve the park's outstanding resources and enhance the visitor's experience. The emphasis is on conservation, preservation, and education. Friends was founded in 1989; over the years, their projects have included trail work, clean-ups, facilities maintenance, tree planting, fund-raising, and the installation of interpretive exhibits. The organization provides a toll-free number for visitor information and sponsors an adopt-a-trail program.

Visitors from distant states as well as nearby residents are encouraged to "befriend" the Blue Ridge Parkway; memberships start at $25. Check out the Friends' website at www.blueridge friends.org. Or contact Friends of the Blue Ridge Parkway at P.O. Box 20986, Roanoke, VA 24018; (800) 228-7275.

## SHENANDOAH NATIONAL PARK

Shenandoah National Park, one of the most popular parks in the country, lies astride the Blue Ridge at the northern end of the Parkway. This skinny park varies in width from 1 to 13 miles and covers almost 200,000 acres, 95% of which is forest and 40% of which is federally designated wilderness. The 105-mile Skyline Drive rides the ridge, traveling the entire length of the park and providing access to facilities and viewpoints. The Shenandoah River and the Massanutten Mountains lie to the west; the Piedmont to the east.

Shenandoah is a Native American name. Some say it means "daughter of the stars". Another interpretation is "river of high mountains". Either name is an apt description of the long, narrow park on the crest of the mountains. A trip through Shenandoah along the Skyline Drive is a ride across the top of Virginia.

Two federal projects were instrumental in the development of Shenandoah National Park, even before it was officially established. One was the Skyline Drive, which was planned to generate jobs in the economically depressed area. President Herbert Hoover authorized the use of drought relief funds for its construction, which began in 1931. The second was the CCC, which contributed a great deal to Shenandoah. Following the CCC's creation in 1933, ten camps were established in the area. The Corp's men were given responsibility for firefighting, erosion control, trail and road construction, infrastructure such as telephone and water service, and planting trees and bushes in open areas and on the roadside along the entire Skyline Drive.

Shenandoah was approved by Congress in 1926 as a site for a large Southern national park. However, while federal funds had been used to build the Skyline Drive and fund CCC projects in the area, no federal monies were appropriated for building the park. Western parks had been established on federal land, but populated private lands had never before been designated for a park. Consequently, there was no precedent for such a purchase, which had to be made with donated funds.

The campaign to create and fund the park involved the untiring efforts of thousands of private citizens, as well as many employees of the state of Virginia. Senator Harry F. Byrd was an enthusiastic supporter. A total of $1.3 million was pledged by Virginia's citizens, and the state legislature added another $1 million. A great deal of partisan lobbying went into the site selection for the park. George Freeman Pollock, an entrepreneur and owner of the Skyland resort in northern Virginia, was influential in the selection. His enthusiasm and energy were tremendous assets in the effort to have the final site chosen. Finally, after years of fights and lawsuits, the state of Virginia had clear title to more than 250 square miles of the Blue Ridge Mountains. Virginia presented this land to the United States on December 12, 1935. The park was dedicated by President Roosevelt on July 3, 1936.

Entrance stations at four different points unofficially split the park into north, central, and south districts. The north district of the park is close to Washington, D.C., and many visitors enter there. The central district contains the park's primary overnight lodging accommodations (and most of its waterfalls). The south district offers much of the beautiful backcountry that Shenandoah is known for. Some facilities are open year-round, but the majority operate from mid-May through late October.

The park includes 500 miles of hiking trails, varying in length from leg-stretchers to 101 miles of the Appalachian Trail, and the waterfall hikes are some of the most popular. The Skyline Drive runs roughly parallel to the Appalachian Trail, and many hikers consider this portion of the Appalachian Trail to be one of the most beautiful. Additionally, there is enough backcountry to keep the backpacker busy for a long while.

The forest, primarily oak and hickory, is an ecosystem with many life forms. The flora include rose azaleas, lady's slipper orchids, jack-in-the-pulpits, interrupted ferns, and over 1,300 other plants. Animal life abounds in the park as well. White-tailed deer, which visitors see frequently, wild turkey, and black bear call the park home. Of the 200 species of birds recorded in the park, you may see some of the permanent residents like ruffed grouse, barred owls, and woodpeckers.

Often called a gentle wilderness, Shenandoah National Park offers many unique areas. One of the most unusual is the large plateau known as Big Meadows, located at an elevation of 3,500 feet. Big Meadows has the greatest variety of plant life in the park, with at least 300 species, and also a wide variety of animal life. At Big Meadows, you'll find a lodge and campground, as well as a gift shop, camp store, gas station, and several of the waterfall trailheads.

Other areas of the park offer their own unrivaled features. At Big Devils Stairs, you can find some of the oldest trees, which are inaccessible to timbering. Hawksbill, at 4,051 feet, is the highest point in the park and contains remnant red spruce and balsam fir forests. Painted trillium await at Laurel Prong. If you climb the ridge trail of popular Old Rag Mountain, you will stand on granite boulders that are part of the basement rock that was formed 1.1 billion years ago.

The park features two visitor centers, an information center, five campgrounds, and seven picnic areas. Stop at the Byrd Visitor Center at Big Meadows (milepost 51) for information and to learn about the park's natural and cultural history. The park entrance fee, which is good for seven days, is $10 per vehicle.

## GREAT SMOKY MOUNTAINS NATIONAL PARK

Located at the southern end of the Blue Ridge Parkway, the Great Smoky Mountains National Park is filled with hiking trails, beautiful campsites, scenic cycling paths, and rivers for fishing and tubing.

The Great Smoky Mountains are part of the Blue Ridge Mountains and the Cherokee called the area Shaconage, "place of blue smoke." The bluish mist that pervades the valleys and hovers over the Blue Ridge Mountains is even more visible in the Smokies, creating a mysterious and eerie hue.

The Cherokee Indians were the first inhabitants of the Great Smoky Mountains. While geologists have developed theories about how the mountains were formed, the Cherokee have another version. Legend has it that a great buzzard was sent down from the sky to find a dry place for everyone to live. Over Cherokee land, the buzzard became very weary and dropped close to the earth. His beating wings struck the soft earth, forming the mountains and valleys and creating the tribe's homeland.

What nature, or a legendary buzzard, so miraculously created, people endangered. Heavy logging stripped the Smokies of vegetation and choked the streams with silt. Brook trout and many other native animals were threatened as a result.

A St. Louis librarian named Horace Kephart was one of the first to recognize the value of the Great Smoky Mountains. He came to the Great Smokies in 1904 to recover from ill health and grew to love the mountains. Appalled by the wide-scale decimation of the land, Kephart worked doggedly for years to have the Smokies preserved as a national park. In *Our Southern Highlands,* he wrote of his years in Deep Creek, Hazel Creek, and Bryson City. His sensitive writing helped alert the public to the fact that the mountains were being destroyed.

In 1923, Mr. and Mrs. Willis P. Davis and Colonel David Chapman of Knoxville, Tennessee, formed the Great Smoky Mountains Conservation Association. Under the leadership of Colonel Chapman, and with the influence of others such as Horace Kephart, groups in North Carolina and Tennessee began to raise money to buy the land. Businessman and philanthropist John D. Rockefeller contributed $5 million to the cause. With the help of all these contributors, Great Smoky Mountains National Park was established on June 15, 1934.

Like Shenandoah, Great Smoky Mountains National Park incorporated private land, which had to be purchased from individuals. Once again, there were many questions concerning titles and right-of-way. Finally, the park was officially dedicated by President Franklin Roosevelt on September 2, 1940.

The park sits astride the border of North Carolina and Tennessee. Elevations range from 840 feet at the mouth of Abrams Creek to 6,642 feet at Clingmans Dome. There are over 800 miles of trails and footpaths, including 70 miles of the Appalachian Trail. These pathways thread through the park, leading to coves, balds, and rushing streams, as well as to dozens of waterfalls. This book includes several waterfall hikes accessed out of Bryson City and Cherokee.

From the Blue Ridge Parkway on the North Carolina side of the park, the first stop is the Oconaluftee Visitor Center, which is open year-round. Here, you can get park information and literature about the Smokies. Adjacent to the visitor center is the Mountain Farm Museum, an exhibit that shows how the mountains' first settlers lived. Just north of the visitor center on Newfound Gap Road, Mingus Mill, a large, water-powered grist mill, grinds corn daily from mid-March through October.

"Always clear and fragrant," wrote Horace Kephart about the forests of the Smokies, and so they are. The park is a sanctuary, preserving some of the world's finest examples of temperate deciduous forest. Over 130 species of trees grow in the Smokies. Broadleaf trees dominate in the coves, and conifer forests cover the crests at the highest elevations. This is the largest remaining virgin forest of the eastern American wilderness, covering an estimated 100,000 acres, or 20% of the park. Of the old-growth forest that remains in the eastern United States, 90% lies within the Great Smoky Mountains National Park.

The park itself takes in nearly 800 square miles. Within its boundaries, there is a wealth of natural wonders. The annual rainfall in the park is over 85 inches at the higher elevations, equivalent to that of a rain forest. This abundant rainfall and the fertile soil have encouraged the development of a world-renowned variety of flora, with more than 1,500 kinds of flowering plants. Many plants in the higher elevations are more typical of New England and Canada than of the southeastern United States.

An additional attraction is the diversity of animal life. There are more than 400 species of animals, including 200 species of birds. The park is this country's salamander capital, with 30 species. There are at least 60 species of mammals, including bear, deer, and wild boar. The wild boar, however, are not a native species and pose a threat to the ecosystem. Their wallowing behavior destroys soil-level plant life, including rare species and even the nests and eggs of ground-nesting birds. Park officials are working to remove these animals.

The United Nations has designated the Great Smoky Mountains National Park as an International Biosphere Reserve because of its abundance and variety of plant and animal life. The park is managed by the National Park Service as a natural and wild environment.

## WATERFALLS

Of all the many treasures to be found in these two national parks and along the Parkway, the most precious are the water resources. The Blue Ridge is laced with many miles of rivers and streams. In essence, the mountains exist because of water. They were molded by the force of water, and water continues to sculpt the valleys and ridges. The nature and personality of the Blue Ridge Mountains are intrinsically tied to the mystery and magic of the water.

We came to reseach the waterfalls of the Blue Ridge; we learned about the complex interrelationship between modern civilization and nature. Millions of years

*Indian Creek Falls, Deep Creek Trail*

of evolution determined the type of plant and animal life that would survive in this region. Native Americans dwelt here for centuries and settlers from far and wide became hardy Appalachian pioneers. The ecological and cultural sights abound on the waterfall trails of the Blue Ridge Mountains.

We came to see the waterfalls, and we found the Blue Ridge Parkway, that undulating ribbon of highway that connects two national parks. The road exists as a monument to men who were committed to providing us all with a view from the mountaintops.

We came to see the waterfalls, and we discovered the Shenandoah National Park and the Great Smoky Mountains National Park. These parks are being preserved because people are waking up to the possibility of losing our valuable resources.

We came to see the waterfalls, and we take away a sense of the mystery and majesty of the mountains. Come and see the waterfalls of the Blue Ridge yourself. Enjoy the peace that the mountains offer. Take a moment to consider the abundant beauty at hand and the long-range wisdom of preserving all of this for future generations.

*And, by all means, share the joy. . .*

VIRGINIA WATERFALLS

SECTION *two*

# one LURAY & SHENANDOAH NATIONAL PARK

**W**HEN THE TIME CAME to decide on a location for the headquarters of Shenandoah National Park, the National Park Service selected Luray. An administrative history report explains that Luray was selected because its townspeople were the earliest and most enthusiastic supporters of the project. Luray's location also added to its appeal. The town lies on US 211, 9 miles west of the entrance to the park's central district.

When the people living within the park were resettled, many moved to Luray and nearby communities. In turn, the park employed people from Luray. The town provided mail service, and farms in the valley supplied staples to those working in the mountains. The park offices were first located downtown, then moved in 1940 to the outskirts, 5 miles east of Luray on US 211.

In the early 1700s, Lt. Governor Alexander Spotswood and the Knights of the Golden Horseshoe ventured through the area. Pioneers began homesteading in the county by the mid-1700s. Luray, the county seat of Page County, was established in 1812 and incorporated in 1871.

Several sources link the name of the town to the Indian word Lorrain, which loosely translates to "crooked waters." But the information sheet "Facts about Luray, Virginia," printed by the Luray–Page County Chamber of Commerce, tells a different story. The Marie family, who were the first settlers in the area, named the town after their grandparents' home–Luray, France.

The county's elevation rises to over 4,000 feet in the mountains of the Blue Ridge and drops to almost 600 feet at the banks of the South Fork of the Shenandoah River, which flows west of town. This historic river may be experienced from a canoe or an inner tube. Several outfitters offer daily trips from April through

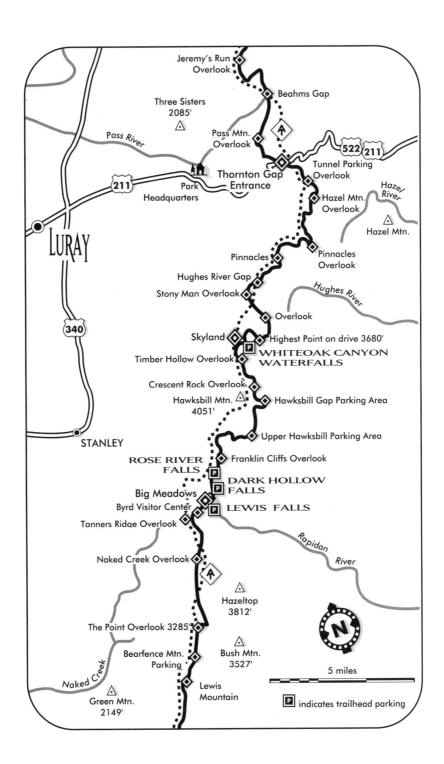

Jeremy's Run Overlook

Beahms Gap

Three Sisters 2085'

Pass River

Pass Mtn. Overlook

522 211

Tunnel Parking Overlook

211

Park Headquarters

Thornton Gap Entrance

Hazel Mtn. Overlook

Hazel River

Hazel Mtn.

LURAY

340

Pinnacles

Pinnacles Overlook

Hughes River Gap

Stony Man Overlook

Hughes River

Overlook

Skyland

Highest Point on drive 3680'

WHITEOAK CANYON WATERFALLS

Timber Hollow Overlook

Crescent Rock Overlook

Hawksbill Mtn. 4051'

Hawksbill Gap Parking Area

Upper Hawksbill Parking Area

STANLEY

ROSE RIVER FALLS

Franklin Cliffs Overlook

DARK HOLLOW FALLS

Big Meadows

Byrd Visitor Center

LEWIS FALLS

Tanners Ridge Overlook

Rapidan River

Naked Creek Overlook

Hazeltop 3812'

The Point Overlook 3285'

Bearfence Mtn. Parking

Bush Mtn. 3527'

Naked Creek

Lewis Mountain

Green Mtn. 2149'

N

5 miles

P indicates trailhead parking

October. You can choose an all-day paddle on beginner-level whitewater or a half-day float on flatwater.

While the county supports poultry and cattle farms and a few small businesses, Luray flourishes as a tourist town, often referred to as the travel center of the Northern Shenandoah Valley. This is due in part to Luray Caverns, the largest and most popular network of caves in the East, with about 500,000 visitors each year. Luray Caverns also carries the distinction of being a U.S. Natural Landmark.

This underground world lies beneath the Shenandoah Valley. It was discovered in 1878, by Andrew Campbell and Benton Stebbins, using only a rope and a candlestick. Luray Caverns, a series of rooms linked together by passageways, contains stalactites and stalagmites, cascades and crystal pools, immense columns, and interesting formations. Saturated with color, this example of nature's handiwork rivals much of the scenery above ground.

Open every day of the year, Luray Caverns offers one-hour tours, scheduled every 20 minutes. Guides lead you to features like the Wishing Well, where millions of coins are collected annually and donated to national health organizations, and the Great Stalacpipe Organ, the world's largest musical instrument. The Organ is explained in a brochure for Luray Caverns. "Stalactites, tuned to concert pitch and accuracy, are struck by electronically controlled, rubber-tipped plungers to produce music of symphonic quality." Credit for this brilliant creation goes to inventor Leland W. Sprinkle.

In addition to exploring the caverns, the grounds host the Car and Carriage Caravan and the Luray Singing Tower. The first is a fascinating museum devoted to the history of transportation. The second is a carillon that serenades the locals with 47 bells.

The Caravan's antique car collection totals over 100, including a distinguished exhibit of some of the oldest cars in the country—all still running. To name a few: 1892 Benz, 1906 Ford, 1907 Buick, 1908 Baker Electric, 1911 Hupmobile, and 1913 Stanley Steamer.

The Tower sings from March through October. Carillonneur David Breneman conducts recitals that last almost an hour. The bells of the carillon range in weight from 12.5 pounds to 7,640 pounds!

If you plan to stay in Luray, try the Luray Caverns Motels, two buildings conveniently located at either entrance to the Caverns. The historic Mimslyn Hotel, the Grand Old Inn of Virginia, awaits with 50 rooms, while Yogi Bear's Jellystone Park and Camp Resort offers shaded trailer and tent sites, as well as cabins.

If you only have a little time to spare, head straight for the Skyline Drive. Shenandoah's central district has two recreation areas with wonderful camping and lodging facilities–Skyland (mileposts 41.7 and 42.5) and Big Meadows (mileposts 51 and 51.2)–which are described in detail under the waterfall descriptions.

Your first stop should be Thornton Gap Entrance Station, via US 211 at milepost 31.5. The entrance fee to the park is $10 per vehicle. Thornton Gap lies at 2,304 feet and a trail leads up another 1,200 feet to Mary's Rocks for a terrific view east and west of the Skyline Drive. You will also find souvenirs, crafts, snacks, and rest room facilities.

Head south on the Skyline Drive to enjoy the waterfalls of the central district of Shenandoah National Park. There are about 15 major waterfalls in the park and most of them are in this area. The waterfalls are listed in this guide in the order you will encounter them traveling south on the Skyline Drive. If you need more information during your travels, stop in at the Byrd Visitor Center at milepost 51. Or get a copy of *Hikes to Waterfalls in Shenandoah National Park* by Joanne Amberson. This guidebook is published by the Shenandoah National Park Association and is available at www.snpbooks.org.

# WATERFALLS IN WHITEOAK CANYON

**FIRST WATERFALL:** 4.6 MILES ROUND-TRIP, STRENUOUS

**ALL WATERFALLS:** 7.2 MILES ROUND-TRIP, STRENUOUS)

Cutting a deep canyon on its way down the mountainside, Whiteoak Run boasts a 1.3-mile stretch with six waterfalls. Numbers, rather than names, denote each waterfall. Dropping 86 feet, Whiteoak Falls #1 is the second highest in the park–shorter than the northern district's Overall Run Falls by five feet.

Park literature lists the heights of the other falls as follows: #2 is 62 feet; #3 is 35 feet; #4 is 41 feet; #5 is 49 feet; and #6 is 60 feet. The heights of the falls add up to 333 feet, but from the trailhead, the blue-blazed Whiteoak Canyon Trail drops 2,000 feet before reaching Whiteoak Falls #6.

The trailhead is located along the Skyline Drive near a resort called Skyland. George Freeman Pollock, a colorful man and a born entrepreneur who established Skyland, came to the area from Washington, D.C., in the 1880s. His mountain retreat began as a tent camp, and log cottages later replaced tents.

*Whiteoak Canyon Falls #1*

Today, Skyland is one of the main concession operations in the park. The north entrance to Skyland sits at 3,680 feet, the highest point of the Skyline Drive. You can stay at motel-like units or rent a rustic cabin. Facilities include a conference hall, a gift shop, and a restaurant that offers mountain cuisine and live entertainment. In season, the Skyland stables provide daily rides on a network of horse trails.

Within the first mile of the trail, you will cross a branch of Whiteoak Run, the Limberlost Trail, the Old Rag Fire Road, and the Limberlost Trail again. Limberlost, an area covered in huge hemlock trees, was named by Pollock and his wife, Addie Nairn, after the novel *Girl of the Limberlost* by Gene Stratton Porter. Addie paid loggers *not* to cut the hemlock, and the biggest trees may be 350–400 years old. Today, however, the hemlock are threatened by of an infestation of the hemlock woolly adelgid. You can also access the 1.3-mile Limberlost Loop Trail from milepost 43.

After Limberlost, the trail becomes steeper, converging with and then crossing Whiteoak Run. Pollock used to bring guests here for his famous barbeque in the old Skyland days. Just beyond the junction with the Skyland-Meadows Horse Trail, a rock overlook affords a good view of the first waterfall (at 2.3 miles).

As you switchback down the steep canyon, occasional views of the other falls open up. You must look carefully to catch every waterfall. After crossing a side creek, the trail cuts in close to the creek just below Whiteoak Falls #6.

The canyon, the run, and the waterfalls were named for the surrounding white oak trees. Ash and tulip also provide shade. Because of heavy use and the sensitive nature of the area, camping is prohibited between Whiteoak Falls #1 and the junction with Cedar Run Link Trail, beyond Whiteoak Falls #6.

DIRECTIONS: **From Luray, head east on US 211 for about 9 miles into the Shenandoah National Park at the Thornton Gap Entrance Station (milepost 31.5). Travel south on the Skyline Drive to milepost 42.6. Whiteoak Canyon Parking Area is on the right, across from the south entrance to Skyland. The trailhead is at the upper end of the parking area.**

*Whiteoak Canyon Falls #2*

# ROSE RIVER FALLS

$\Big[$ 2.6 MILES ROUND-TRIP, MODERATE $\Big]$

Rose River Falls, although not the tallest, is one of the prettiest in the park. The 67-foot drop falls in a series of cascades, and is especially impressive after a heavy rain. The hike takes you through a beautiful hardwood forest, with oaks and maples, as well as trailside wildflowers in the spring.

While you can return after reaching the falls in 1.3 miles, you can also continue for a longer hike, completing the circuit of Rose River Loop Trail (totaling 4 miles). A 0.2-mile side trail off the loop leads to Dark Hollow Falls (see next waterfall entry). Ask at the Byrd Visitor Center (milepost 51) for information/maps in order to hike this loop and visit two of Shenandoah's waterfalls.

To reach Rose River Falls, cross the Skyline Drive from the north end of the parking area and follow the Rose River Fire Road east about 100 feet. At the trail post, pick up the Rose River Loop Trail, which is to the left. You will share this yellow-blazed trail with horse traffic (which has the right-of-way) for the next 0.5 mile. When the horse trail veers left, keep straight on the blue-blazed trail. At about the 1-mile point, the trail takes a sharp right and soon parallels the river. There are several good viewing spots along the trail.

DIRECTIONS: **From Luray, travel to the Skyline Drive (see directions under Whiteoak Canyon) and go south to milepost 49.4. Fishers Gap Overlook is on the right, and the fire road crosses the Skyline Drive at the north end of the parking area.**

# DARK HOLLOW FALLS

$\Big[$ 1.4 MILES ROUND-TRIP, MODERATE $\Big]$

The park's shortest trail that leads to a waterfall follows Hogcamp Branch to Dark Hollow Falls. The length of this waterfall trail and the location of the trailhead, across from the Byrd Visitor Center, make Dark Hollow Falls Trail one of the most popular in the park. While short, it still includes a steep uphill return walk.

Before beginning this hike, stop in at the Byrd Visitor Center, which houses interpretive displays and where you can obtain information and maps. The center is named after Harry F. Byrd, Sr., a Virginia governor and U.S. senator who helped to raise funds to purchase land for the park. He climbed his favorite mountain, Old Rag, every year.

North across the Skyline Drive from the visitor center, you'll find the trailhead for Dark Hollow Falls, at an elevation of 3,490 feet. The blue-blazed trail takes you across the branch on a stone bridge and descends steeply along the left bank to the top of the falls. Then head away from the branch, and back, to reach an observation platform at the top. Another 0.1 mile downstream, you'll reach an excellent viewpoint at the base of the falls. The narrow cascade courses 70 feet over a series of terraced drops. Hogcamp Branch flows into the Rose River downstream.

The cascading waterfall flows over greenstone, a reminder of activity that occurred hundreds of millions of years ago. Greenstone is metamorphosed lava. This rock tops much of the crest of the Blue Ridge and can be seen at several places in the park, including Stony Man and Hawksbill Mountain.

**DIRECTIONS: From Luray, travel to the Skyline Drive (see directions under Whiteoak Canyon) and go south to milepost 50.7. Dark Hollow Parking Area is on the left, just north of Big Meadows. The trailhead is at the north end of the parking area.**

# LEWIS FALLS [3.3-MILE LOOP, STRENUOUS]

Lewis Falls Trail, one of the many spurs along the famous Appalachian Trail, combines with a 1-mile stretch of the Appalachian Trail to create a wonderful loop hike to Lewis Falls. The approximately 2,160-mile Appalachian Trail, which runs from Mount Katahdin in Maine to Springer Mountain in Georgia, has its longest single-state section (536 miles) in Virginia, and 101 of those miles are located in the park.

Lewis Falls Trail (blue blazes), which you reach from the Appalachian Trail behind the amphitheater, descends about 1 mile to the falls. A spur trail (150 feet to the left) brings you to a viewing area near the top of Lewis Falls, a sheer drop of 81 feet. The creek originates at Lewis Spring (enclosed) near the point where this loop picks up the Appalachian Trail. Lewis Spring eventually flows into Hawksbill Creek.

Past the falls, a rugged section of trail leads mostly uphill to a service road. Turn right and hike a short distance to pick up the Appalachian Trail (white blazes) on the left. The 1-mile stretch of the Appalachian Trail passes under Blackrock, elevation 3,721 feet. If you climb up to Blackrock, you can look out over the Shenandoah Valley and the Massanutten Mountains, as well as the distant Alleghenies.

Big Meadows, the location of the trailhead, sits 1 mile off the Skyline Drive. This recreation site offers a lodge and dining room, a gift shop, an amphitheater, a camp store, a restaurant, picnic grounds, and the largest campground in the park. It was at Big Meadows that President Roosevelt dedicated Shenandoah National Park.

Big Meadows gets its name from the beautiful grassy opening, the largest open area in the park. Centuries ago, American Indians either found a natural clearing, the result of a lightning-induced fire, or they cleared it. Whatever the case, they probably took advantage of the opening as a hunting and camping area. Early settlers may have expanded the clearing for cattle grazing. By the early 1900s, Big Meadows was a combination of meadow and pasture. Today the park is keeping 137 acres open, and the rest is reverting to forest.

DIRECTIONS: **From Luray, travel to the Skyline Drive (see directions under Whiteoak Canyon) and go south to milepost 51, Big Meadow. At the visitor center, you can get maps, brochures, and information. Then drive to the picnic area and park; locate the trail behind the amphitheater.**

# two WAYNESBORO

**W**AYNESBORO IS LOCATED at the northern end
of the Blue Ridge Parkway in the center of the eastern portion of the
Shenandoah Valley. At Rockfish Gap on Interstate 64, the Blue Ridge Parkway
meets the Shenandoah National Park's Skyline Drive. The Allegheny Mountains lie
to the west, and the crests of the Blue Ridge flank the valley's eastern edge.

This part of Virginia, sometimes called the crossroads of the Shenandoah
Valley, is often deemed the state's crowning glory—and for good reason. From the
grandeur of the mountaintops to the richness of the valley below, the area offers
breathtaking vistas, plenty of outdoor recreation, and many historical and cultural
attractions.

The first white man thought to have viewed the area was a German
explorer named John Lederer. In 1669, he gazed upon the Shenandoah Valley from
atop the Blue Ridge Mountains and reported his findings of rich, fertile land to the
governor in Williamsburg. Soon, frontier farms and villages were established by
Scotch, German, Irish, and English settlers.

Waynesboro was originally part of a 1736 land grant from King George II
of England to Governor William Gooch. Gooch transferred the land to William Beverly. In 1739, Beverly granted 465 acres to Joseph Tees, the proprietor of Tees Tav-
ern, and the village of Teesville was formed on the west bank of the South River.
After the Revolutionary War, the town's name was changed to Waynesborough
(later shortened to Waynesboro) in honor of the flamboyant General "Mad"
Anthony Wayne. Wayne was famous for his reckless courage in combat.

More than half a century later, Basic City was founded on the east side of
the South River. Waynesboro and Basic City consolidated in 1924, and industrial
growth brought an increase in population. By February of 1948, Waynesboro was the
25th city in Virginia's history to be designated a city of the first class under the terms
of the state constitution.

For the art enthusiast, Waynesboro serves up a full plate. The new state
craft center, the Artisans Center of Virginia, recently opened in Waynesboro near
Exit 94 of Interstate 64 and features the fine crafts of over 180 Virginia artisans. The
wide array of beautiful handcrafted items on display includes pottery, glass, wood,
metal, basketry, woven and quilted items, paper, jewelry, and much more. Admission

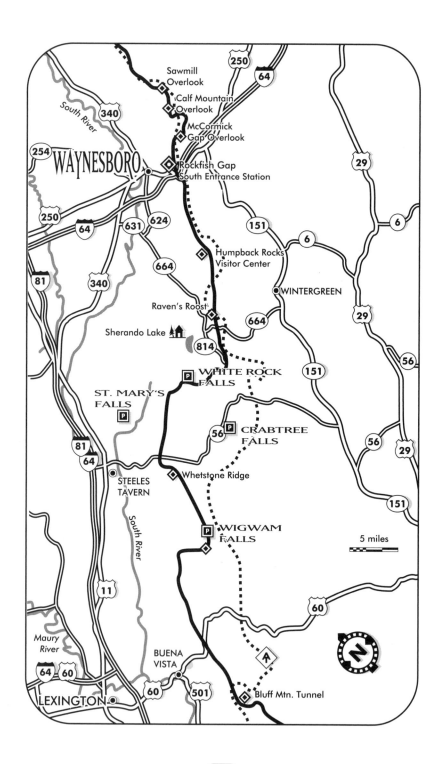

is free to both the state's collection and exhibitions. Classes are offered on a seasonal basis for children, beginners, and professional craftsmen.

The Shenandoah Valley Art Center, a nonprofit organization staffed by volunteers, is dedicated to promoting the arts in the Shenandoah Valley. In addition to being a showcase for outstanding artists from the region, the center also features exhibits, performances, workshops, and classes in the various creative arts. The center is located at 600 West Main Street, and admission is free.

The works of P. Buckley Moss are housed in the aptly named P. Buckley Moss Museum (also free). Moss's paintings are widely recognized throughout the country. This internationally known artist is famous for her inimitable style, symbolism, and unique portrayal of the simple lifestyles of the Amish and Mennonite people. The museum is located at 150 P. Buckley Moss Drive in a building that resembles the style of houses built in the early 1800s by settlers of this area.

One of the most outstanding art events in Waynesboro is the Fall Foliage Festival. Held in downtown Waynesboro in early October, the festival draws more than 200 artisans from all over who display their pottery, metalwork, paintings, photographs, sculpture, and jewelry. The show is reputed to be one of the best such events in the eastern U.S., and the grandeur of the fall foliage surrounding the Shenandoah Valley can't be beat.

A favorite shop, Virginia Metalcrafters, produces some of colonial America's finest brass and iron pieces. An observation booth at the factory allows visitors to watch the artisans using the original technique of pouring molten brass into hand-formed sand molds. Many of the accessories found in Colonial Williamsburg are authentically reproduced here.

Waynesboro is centrally located to many historic landmarks. Thomas Jefferson's Monticello and James Monroe's Ashlawn-Highland are both in Charlottesville, within a 30-minute drive from town. Stonewall Jackson's home and Lee Chapel, museum and burial place of Robert E. Lee, are 30 minutes south. Founded in 1877, the Fishburne Military School is a State and National Historic Landmark. Fishburne occupies the largest privately owned tract of land adjacent to downtown Waynesboro.

The Woodrow Wilson birthplace, an 1846 Greek Revival townhouse in nearby Staunton, is listed as a National Historic Landmark. Some of the original furnishings are still in place, including the crib where Wilson slept as a baby, and the family Bible where the former president's birth is recorded. Staunton's newly opened Shenandoah Shakespeare Theater gives Shakespearean performances a whole new vitality. In downtown Staunton, the authentic replica of the Black Friar's Theater truly takes the audience back in time.

The Frontier Culture Museum offers a unique glimpse into the past of this colorful region. Also located in Staunton, this living museum presents working farms that illustrate the European influence on America's eighteenth- and nineteenth-century culture. Interpreters in costume demonstrate the German, Northern Irish, and English impact on life in colonial America. The museum conducts programs daily, except on Thanksgiving, Christmas, and New Year's Day.

While fascinating, the man-made attractions of the Waynesboro area pale in comparison with what nature has to offer. From the Blue Ridge Parkway, you can access George Washington National Forest and the Appalachian Trail. In 1998, the Pedlar Ranger District of George Washington National Forest administratively merged with the Glenwood Ranger District of Jefferson National Forest. Their joint office is in Natural Bridge Station.

The Park Service operates the Sherando Lake Recreation Area, where you'll find a campground and picnic grounds. Located in the mountains about 14 miles south of Waynesboro, the area can be accessed from the Parkway at milepost 16 (4.5 miles south on VA 814). The majority of the facilities are located between two lakes, the largest of which (24 acres) was built by the Civilian Conservation Corps in the 1930s. The upper lake, used primarily for fishing, covers seven acres. Sherando Lake Recreation Area makes a good base for a variety of waterfall hikes.

Just 4 miles east of Waynesboro at Rockfish Gap, the southern entrance to the Skyline Drive (milepost 105.4) meets the northernmost point of the Blue Ridge Parkway (milepost 0). At Rockfish Gap Tourist Information Center, the helpful volunteer staff will assist you and answer your questions about the Shenandoah Valley, the Skyline Drive, the Blue Ridge Parkway, and other area attractions, making it an ideal place to get your bearings and plan your stay. All of the directions to the waterfalls described under Waynesboro start from Rockfish Gap.

# WHITE ROCK FALLS

[ 1.8 MILES ROUND-TRIP, MODERATE ]

White Rock Falls Trail was built in 1979 by the Youth Conservation Corps. The trail is maintained by members of the Tidewater Appalachian Trail Club, who volunteer their time to do upkeep and repair on 10+ miles of the Appalachian Trail–from Reeds Gap to the Tye River. The club adopted the White

Rock Falls Trail even though it isn't part of the Appalachian Trail, and member Bob Adkisson took to regularly removing fallen or encroaching vegetation.

Begin at Slacks Overlook (2,800 feet), and after three creek crossings–a foot bridge and two rock hops–savor the view of the White Rock Creek Valley from the rocky outcropping. One switchback will take you below the outcropping where there is a small sign tacked to a tree. It says "falls," indicating the waterfall is straight ahead. (White Rock Falls Trail takes a sharp right and continues 1.7 miles to milepost 18.5, White Rock Gap.) This yellow-blazed trail doesn't stray more than 0.5 mile from the Parkway, yet it is impossible to hear any car noise–just the sounds of the forest.

White Rock Falls is a small-volume waterfall, but it spills 30 feet into an incredible gorge. The walls of the narrow canyon embrace you on three sides, old growth hemlock trees tower above. Although the creek is small, the pool at the base of the falls is big enough to enjoy a swim.

Downstream, White Rock Creek flows into the North Fork of the Tye River. There is a community named White Rock, a half dozen houses, located at the convergence of the two creeks. The white rock refered to in the creek and town names is the quartz that is so prevalent in the area.

DIRECTIONS: **From Waynesboro, get on the Blue Ridge Parkway at milepost 0 and head south to milepost 19.9, Slacks Overlook (on the right). To find the trailhead, go across the road and walk north for about 60 yards. There is a wooden sign (look down the slope towards the woods) marking the trailhead.**

# ST. MARY'S WATERFALL

[4.4 MILES ROUND-TRIP, EASY]

St. Mary's Waterfall is in St. Mary's Wilderness, part of George Washington National Forest. The wilderness tract is over 10,000 acres, making it one of the largest wilderness areas in Virginia. The Virginia Wilderness Bill of 1984 established that all roads in the St. Mary's Wilderness must be closed to vehicles and commercial activity. St. Mary's continues to allow only foot traffic within its boundaries.

The area's elevation varies from 1,700 to 3,600 feet. The highest point is Cellar Mountain, which has rocky bluffs near the base. Surprisingly, the area was never logged. You will find that oak and hickory rule the forest, but you won't find big trees because the soil is not sufficient and the inclines are too rugged. Other vegetation includes sumac, black birch, rhododendron, laurel, and our favorite,

*St Mary's Waterfall*

blueberries. St. Mary's River and its tributaries contain a large population of native trout and the wild land makes good bear habitat.

The St. Mary's Trail totals 6.2 miles, but the side trail that leads to the waterfall bears off after 1.4 miles. From the barrier gate, hike along the St. Mary's River on an old roadbed and then a dried-up stream. After crossing the river (wading during high water), the St. Mary's Trail bears right and heads toward the crest of the Blue Ridge to Green Pond, a one-acre, high-elevation bog.

Go left instead, through a campsite, and across the St. Mary's River again in order to pick up the 0.8-mile waterfall spur, which leads into the St. Mary's Gorge. The St. Mary's Waterfall spills over a 10-foot ledge between the quartzite walls of this miniature canyon. The large pool at the base is surrounded by jagged boulders and short cliffs.

The historical highlight in the St. Mary's Wilderness is a surface-mining excavation. There is a creek, a trail, and a mountain—all by the name of Mine Bank. For the first 50 years of the last century, several mines in the gorge produced manganese and iron ore. A railroad tramway came up the hollow and carried the ore to processing plants.

Evidence of the mining operation remains in the forest. The topographic map printed by the Forest Service shows four old mine sites located on a section of the St. Mary's Trail beginning less than 1 mile past the waterfall spur. Several trails in this wilderness area follow the former tramline or old mining roads.

Within the boundaries of the St. Mary's Wilderness, there are over 15 miles of trail, including Mine Bank Trail, Bald Mountain Trail, Cellar Mountain Trail, and Cold Springs Trail. Contact the Forest Service for a topographic map with trail system information and special considerations. From the parking lot on Forest Service 41 to 500 feet past the falls, group size is limited to less than 10 people, and camping and fires are not allowed 150 feet from the trail.

**DIRECTIONS: From Waynesboro, get on the Blue Ridge Parkway at milepost 0 and head south to milepost 27.2. Exit onto VA 56 going west (right) and travel 3.6 miles to Vesuvius, where County Road 608 becomes part of VA 56 for about 0.5 mile. Bear right when CR 608 splits off from VA 56, and drive 2.4 miles to a right turn onto Forest Road 41. This road becomes gravel within a few hundred yards and ends at a parking area after 1.4 miles. The trailhead is at the upper end beyond the information board.**

# CRABTREE FALLS

[ **4 MILES ROUND-TRIP, MODERATE** ]

Crabtree Falls might be the highest waterfall east of the Mississippi, depending on how you qualify a waterfall, but there is no doubt that Crabtree Falls is the highest waterfall in Virginia. Crabtree Falls is really a name given to five major waterfalls (and several smaller ones) on Crabtree Creek, which flows into the Tye River. Within 0.5 mile, the creek drops 1,200 feet. There is one vertical drop of 500 feet.

Crabtree Falls is a popular attraction. If you spread out the estimated 20,000 visitors over a year, you'd have about 55 a day. Unfortunately, most people come between May and October. Try squeezing that number into twenty parking spaces. (In March, yours may be the only car in the lot.)

Crabtree Falls is famous for its connection to the well-known television show *The Waltons*. The falls were not shown on television, but the name was mentioned several times during the life of the program, usually in reference to a Sunday outing.

The name Crabtree is thought to have come from William Crabtree, who settled in the area in 1777. Some even say he discovered the waterfall. Another noted pioneer, Allen Tye, who did extensive exploration in the Blue Ridge Mountains, is identified as having discovered the Tye River.

The land at the base of the falls was almost developed as a resort area in the late 1960s. Land owner Hugh D. Bolton put up No Trespassing signs and stated that he wanted to create something called Living Waters. The residents of Nelson County encouraged involvement from the Forest Service, who had purchased acreage around the falls since the 1930s through small acquisitions and land exchanges, acquiring the falls in 1968. In 1972, after many unsuccessful offers to purchase the land at the base of the falls, legal proceedings began to obtain the two tracts.

The land became part of the George Washington National Forest, and Southern District Representative Jay Robinson secured money from Congress to be used to improve the area around the falls. The waterfall trail was since developed into a showpiece of the Pedlar Ranger District. There are wooden stairs, gravel paths, railed overlooks, and a spectacular bridge over the Tye River.

The 110-foot wooden bridge across the Tye has a most interesting story. It was the first of the trail improvements made by the Forest Service in the late 1970s. When we read the cost, we thought it was a misprint–$62,000! Why so much? This beautiful bridge, a laminated arch, was shipped from New York in one piece. Cranes lifted and placed it over the Tye River in 1978.

The trail parallels the Tye River a short distance before crossing on the bridge. Then, the blue-blazed trail follows Crabtree Creek for 3 miles through a sliver of old hemlock, as well as yellow birch, striped maple, and American elm, to Crabtree Meadows. Or, you can turn around at the last waterfall overlook (1.5 miles) for a hike that also totals 3 miles. The first of many observation decks begins only 700 feet past the Tye River.

Crabtree Meadows is an open area with scattered crab apple and apple trees. In the 1930s, several families lived on the site of Crabtree Meadow, a national forest primitive campsite with water and pit toilets. The Appalachian Trail can be accessed from here via a 0.5-mile side trail.

Crabtree Falls has a fascinating history and offers many nice features, but something struck us as most unusual–a pay phone. There is a telephone right after you cross the Tye River–a strange thing to see in the woods. It was put in because of the growing number of accidents at the falls. Rescue numbers are posted inside. There have been 23 deaths (the last one in 2000) and many injuries at Crabtree Falls. The Forest Service even maintains a four-wheel-drive road at the top of the falls primarily for use in rescues.

DIRECTIONS: From Waynesboro, access the Blue Ridge Parkway at milepost 0 and head south to milepost 27.2. Exit onto VA 56 going east (left) and follow the signs to Crabtree Falls (about 6.3 miles). There is a paved parking area on the right and the trail begins at the upper end. To reach Crabtree Meadows, head back towards the Parkway for 2.8 miles and turn left onto Forest Road 826. The upper trailhead is 4 miles down and on the left.

# WIGWAM FALLS [0.4 MILE LOOP, EASY]

The 30-foot Wigwam Falls is convenient to the Blue Ridge Parkway and requires only a short hike. It is worth a visit if you are up on the Parkway, but it is nothing like Crabtree Falls, the area's most spectacular waterfall.

To reach Wigwam Falls, follow the easy and short Yankee Horse Trail on the east side of the Parkway through open hardwood forest. The waterfall isn't actually on Wigwam Creek, but on a small tributary, which can just about dry up in the summer. In the winter, you can see Wigwam Falls from the road.

An interesting part of visiting this waterfall is learning about the logging in the area and seeing the 200-foot reconstructed track of an old railroad. This narrow-gauge line was part of the Irish Creek Railway, built by the South River Lumber Company to access trees that were untouched until the early 1900s. The area was logged out by the late 1930s.

The name given the trail–Yankee Horse–has a story behind it. This area was visited by Stonewall Jackson's troops during the Civil War. Supposedly, a Union soldier's horse fell here and had to be shot. The nearby Wigwam Mountain is said to be an ancient Indian hunting grounds. There is a picnic table and an interpretive sign at this Parkway overlook.

DIRECTIONS: From Waynesboro, get on the Blue Ridge Parkway at milepost 0 and head south to milepost 34.4, Yankee Horse Ridge Parking Area. The trailhead is marked and obvious.

# three GLASGOW

**W**ITH FEW AMENITIES or accommodations, Glasgow doesn't attract the tourist crowd, but the town's best attribute is location. The rural community of Glasgow sits on the western slopes of the Blue Ridge Mountains at the confluence of the Maury River and the James River. The town almost marks the dividing line between Jefferson National Forest and George Washington National Forest.

American Indian tribes inhabited the area for hundreds of years before the first white settlers. In 1670, the main camp of the Monocan Indians was located near Glasgow. The triberuled the Blue Ridge from the north banks of the James River eastward. The first pioneers, mostly Scotsmen, came to the area in the 1730s. One such immigrant, Joseph Glasgow, was a descendant of the Earl of Glasgow; another early resident was John P. Salling. Benjamin Borden owned Glasgow's first piece of land, which subsequently became part of the Salling and Glasgow homesteads. The oldest house in town, built by Peter A. Salling, still stands.

Glasgow was the site of the first battle west of the Blue Ridge between the Iroquois and the early settlers. On December 18, 1742, a skirmish started a series of conflicts that lasted two years. With the Treaty of Lancaster, the Indians gave up the Shenandoah Valley, pushing the fighting with settlers further west.

A real estate boom hit the Shenandoah Valley in the 1890s. Like many towns, Glasgow was a product of this instant growth created by development companies. General Fitzhugh Lee and several other gentlemen who made up the board of directors for the Rockbridge Company built themselves a town.

The company bought land, mapped out lots, and encouraged businesses to move into the area. But like many boomtowns, the story of Glasgow's progress was short-lived and included a power plant that never ran and a hotel that never opened. Today, Glasgow is a quiet town with a population of just over 1,000. The town's 1.5 square miles supports one big company, a textile factory called Burlington Industries. Except for the bank and high school, few other facilities exist in Glasgow. But while the community offers little in the way of craft shops, art galleries, or museums, Glasgow makes an excellent base for visiting the area's waterfalls. Additionally, the larger towns of Lexington and Lynchburg are within an hour's drive.

You can dine at the newly opened restaurant and motel, the Wright Place. This friendly, family-run operation serves guest that often include hikers and

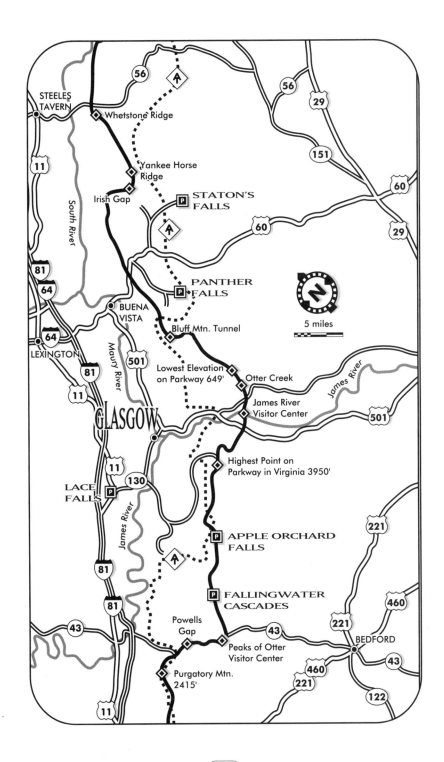

boaters. It was formerly the Blue Ridge Restaurant and Motel. In addition to spending the night there, you can overnight at one of several two-bedroom cottages. Try the Cottage in the Woods or Sallings Mountain Cottage.

Outdoor recreation opportunities abound just outside of town–picnicking, hiking, hunting, swimming, fishing, and boating. The Appalachian Trail leaves George Washington National Forest, crosses US 501, and enters Jefferson National Forest a few miles southeast of Glasgow near the James River Visitor Center (milepost 63.6). Cave Mountain Lake, a seven-acre national forest recreation area, opens in May and provides a bath house, picnic units, and camping through October. A lifeguard monitors swimming on the lake during the summer months. The beach is the length of a football field. Reasonable fees are charged for day and overnight use.

The 8,886-acre James River Face Wilderness was Virginia's first designated wilderness area (in 1975). This special section of national forest, which only allows foot travel, provides a wonderful escape into a typical Appalachian hardwood forest. Climb Highrock Knob (3,073 feet) to reach the highest elevation in the wilderness or hike along the James River (650 feet) to reach the lowest. Balcony Falls Trail, a definite highlight, runs through part of the wilderness area starting from the parking lot at Locher Tract. Views from the ridgetop include the James River Gorge and the town of Glasgow.

The waterfall hikes near Glasgow take you into both national forests. The two waterfalls northeast of town take you into the Pedlar District of George Washington National Forest; and the two waterfalls south of town start on the Blue Ridge Parkway and drop into the Glenwood District of Jefferson National Forest. There is also a small waterfall at the Natural Bridge of Virginia. This popular nearby attraction is worth the visit. So, pick up some picnic foods–a bucket of chicken and a side of slaw–at the corner grill in Glasgow and head out of town. *(Note:* In 1998 the Pedlar Ranger District of George Washington National Forest administratively merged with the Glenwood Ranger District of Jefferson National Forest. Their joint office is located in Natural Bridge Station, a few miles west of Glasgow.)

## STATON'S FALLS   [NO HIKE NECESSARY]

Staton's Falls on Staton's Creek secured its name from a local family. William Staton of Amherst County, an early landowner in the area, may have owned property along the creek. Now the area around the falls is part of the Pedlar Ranger

District of George Washington National Forest. Other names for Staton's Falls include Lace Falls and Deadman's Falls.

The words of Michael T. Shoemaker, from his *Hiking Guide to the Pedlar District* perfectly describe Staton's Falls: "It is composed of several falls and cascades, which when added together descend a great height. The interesting feature of Staton's Falls is not the height, however, but the distinctive zig-zag pattern of the series of falls."

Staton's Falls descends about 140 feet, and the first drop of 15 feet across the road from the parking area. An 80-foot plunge follows immediately as the creek continues to crash through the gorge. Although a hike is not necessary to enjoy this waterfall, you may walk along the road for about 100 yards, scramble down the bank to the creek, and explore other cascades. Your opportunity for adventure here is as extensive as your energy. About 1 mile from the falls, Staton's Creek flows into the Pedlar River.

While driving on Fiddlers Green Way to Staton's Falls, about 0.5 mile before you reach the parking area, there is a small pull off on the left. Two posts indicate the spot where there should be an interpretive sign reading virgin forest. Officials suspect that a fraternity was responsible for stealing the sign.

The interpretive sign designated an area of virgin, or old growth forest. Logging in the early 1900s bypassed this small stand of trees because of the steep hillsides along Staton's Creek. You will find yellow poplar, red oak, white pine, and hemlock. Some of the huge trees measure 5 feet around and 100 feet tall.

DIRECTIONS: **From Glasgow, take US 501 north to Buena Vista and head east on US 60 for about 5 miles to the Blue Ridge Parkway. Continue east past the Parkway on US 60 for 3.2 miles, where you'll see a sign for Oronco and County Road 605 (Pedlar River Road). Turn left and travel 1.7 miles to a fork. Go right onto County Road 633 (Fiddlers Green Way), which immediately turns to gravel. The parking area is 1.1 miles up CR 633 on the right. Walk across the road to the beginning of the falls.**

# PANTHER FALLS ⸱⸱⸱⸱⸱⸱ [1 MILE ROUND-TRIP, EASY]

Panther Falls is on the Pedlar River in the George Washington National Forest. The waterfall's name harkens back to a time when panthers (often called mountain lions) roamed these parts. It would seem, the river's name recalls a time peddlers roamed these parts, too. However, in his Hiking Guide to the Pedlar District, Michael T. Shoemaker states, "Although peddlers were common along the Pedlar River, the river's name derives from the surname of an early settler who drowned in it." And he continues, "The name of the Pedlar River was in use at least as early as 1742."

Panther Falls is often more a party place than a scenic area, because the spot is popular with students from local colleges—even though alcohol is not permitted. The swimming hole below the falls is the primary attraction, and people dive off the boulders surrounding the pool. At certain points, the water is over 20 feet deep, but a sign warns of submerged rocks. Several people have lost their lives here, and the sign states the date of the last death, as well as a warning of strong currents and undertow.

In March, while the tail end of winter blew snow flurries our faces, we were alone at Panther Falls and it was beautiful. The Pedlar River comes around an S-turn and creates an eight-foot wide chute where the river squeezes between two huge boulders. This powerful sluice falls 10 feet into a blue-green pool before sliding over a smaller drop. The forest around the falls is second- and third-growth—about 70 years old.

On the drive to Panther Falls, after turning onto Forest Road 315A, you will pass Robert's Creek Cemetery, one of many old family cemeteries in the Pedlar Ranger District. The cemeteries mark homesites from the pioneer days. Rock piles, terraces, and cleared land show evidence of farming from the late 1700s until the Depression.

Before you reach the gate to begin your hike, a path leads off to the right into a wildlife clearing. Created to add diversity to the woods and attract wildlife, this forest opening offers wonderful primitive camping. Camping is also allowed 150 yards from the river. (Yellow diamond markers attempt to delineate this boundary.)

Begin your hike at the gate. The road here was closed to vehicles in the mid-1980s because of overuse. A gradual descent on the roadbed takes you down to the Pedlar River. Signs tacked on trees read Trout Fishing Waters. The Pedlar River, stocked several times in the spring (and in the fall if the water level cooperates), offers fishing. Since the road to the falls was closed, the grasses and plants have slowly been restored in the large, open area. Follow the river a short distance to the falls.

DIRECTIONS: **From Glasgow, take US 501 north to Buena Vista and head east on US 60 for about 5 miles to the Blue Ridge Parkway. Continue east on US 60, just** past the Parkway, and turn right onto Forest Road 315, a well-graded gravel road. Travel 3.4 miles and turn left onto 315A, a 0.5-mile side road that ends in a parking circle. The trailhead is beyond the wooden information board at the lower end of the parking lot. The trail begins down the old roadbed past the gate.

# LACE FALLS [2 MILES ROUND-TRIP, EASY]

Lace Falls is located at the Natural Bridge of Virginia, the state's famous attraction that claims to be one of the seven wonders of the world. The incredible limestone formation, which is 215 feet high and 90 feet across, definitely upstages this 50-foot waterfall. A brochure states that the bridge "once was the summit of a large waterfall. During the 100 million years Cedar Creek flowed, there were also subterranean passageways in the softer stone under the existing arch, which eventually washed away leaving the harder rock of the structure you see now."

Pick up a map when you arrive and follow the self-guided tour through this Natural Historic Landmark. You will learn about the U.S. president who first owned the Natural Bridge, and you will see another U.S. president's initials carved in the rock. The Monocan Indians believed the bridge, a gift from the Great Spirit, helped their people escape from the Shawnee and Powhattans. According to legend, a canyon interfered with the Indians' retreat, but after kneeling in prayer, a bridge appeared across the canyon. The Monocan Indians called it the Bridge of God.

Start from the gift shop and walk alongside Cascade Creek, with its tumbling waters and small cascades. You will pass a stand of arbor vitae trees, an evergreen in the pine family; the largest trees are 1,000 years old. As the trail turns to the right, descending into the steep ravine formed by Cedar Creek, you get your first view of the Natural Bridge. In addition to this impressive natural wonder, you will pass the creekside Summerhouse Café, the Catheral Wall, the Monocan Indian Village, the Saltpepper Cave, the Hemlock Grove, and the spur to the Lost River Site. This is a most impressive nature trail. The trail ends at a circular observation area where you can view Lace Falls flowing over travertine boulders.

The Natural Bridge of Virginia includes several other attractions, such as an underground cavern, a toy museum, and a wax museum. There is also a hotel, dining room, and gift shop.

DIRECTIONS: From Glasgow, travel west on VA 130 for several miles to VA 11. You can't miss it. The park is open year-round and the admission fee is $10.

# APPLE ORCHARD FALLS

$\left[ \text{2.4 MILES ROUND-TRIP, STRENUOUS} \right]$

On the Blue Ridge Parkway stretch of the drive to Apple Orchard Falls, you will travel from the lowest point on the entire Parkway to the highest point on the Parkway in Virginia. The James River (elevation 668 feet) at milepost 63.7 is only 13 miles from milepost 76.7 (elevation 3,950 feet) near Apple Orchard Overlook.

Apple Orchard Falls flows down the west side of Apple Orchard Mountain (4,225 feet), the second highest peak in Virginia. The orchards on Apple Orchard Mountain are really oak orchards, a form of northern hardwood forest that has been dwarfed by the extreme weather at this high elevation. The stunted northern red oaks and the lack of shrubs create an orchard of sorts that is often mistaken for apple trees.

Apple Orchard Falls Trail begins at Sunset Fields. The grassy clearing and excellent western view attract visitors who want to watch the sun go down. Hike to the falls in the late afternoon, timing your return to catch the sunset over the mountains.

The trail leaves park and enters national forest land within the first 100 yards. From the parking area to the falls, the trail loses 1,000 feet in elevation. You'll intersect the Appalachian Trail and two old logging roads before reaching the creek. There is a foot bridge at the brink of the falls, but you must cross the creek and do the switchbacks before being rewarded with a view.

The 150-foot Apple Orchard Falls, on a small tributary in the Parker Gap watershed, is part of the headwaters of North Creek. The tributary goes over several stair-steps before free falling off a narrow overhang. At the base, it squeezes between huge boulders and flows into an isolated, open valley.

Instead of backtracking, try a one-way, downhill waterfall hike. Continue past the falls for 2.4 miles (another 1,000-foot elevation loss) to Forest Road 59. To place a shuttle car, take Forest Road 812 from the north end of Sunset Fields to Forest Road 768. Turn left and continue to FR 59. The trailhead is to the left at the end of the road.

The area around Apple Orchard Falls Trail was once owned and logged by the Virginia Lumber and Extract Company. The Forest Service bought the land in 1917. A ceremony took place in October of 1987 to dedicate it as a National Recreation Trail.

In the Glenwood Ranger District of Jefferson National Forest, Apple Orchard Falls is part of a special management area that protects the trail and surrounding drainage. This means no cutting! An estimated 500 acres is being set aside to emphasize recreation. Termed an interior forest, the area is a nesting and breeding ground for song birds wintering in Central and South America.

DIRECTIONS: **From Glasgow, take US 501 south and travel 9 miles up to the Blue Ridge Parkway at the James River. Head south on the Parkway for about 14 miles to Sunset Fields Overlook at milepost 78.4. The trailhead is in the middle of the parking area.**

# FALLINGWATER CASCADES
[1.6-MILE LOOP, MODERATE]

Fallingwater Cascades is on a National Recreation Trail that was established, along with Flat Top Trail, in 1982. The trailhead is on the Blue Ridge Parkway, but you will enter the Jefferson National Forest (Glenwood Ranger District) within 50 yards. Stone steps lead down to Fallingwater Creek, and a footbridge signifies the beginning of the falls. The parking area is at 2,557 feet; the waterfall, 2,300 feet.

Fallingwater Creek originates on Chestnut Mountain and flows southwest to form the headwaters of Jenning's Creek. Located in the drainage for Wilkerson Gap, Fallingwater Cascades rushes 200 feet down the ridge. Two dead-end side trails, marked with signs reading 150 feet to view, provide wonderful vantage points of the moderate-volume slide and the surrounding hemlocks and rhododendron.

Along the trail, you will find geologic formations called talus slopes, evidence of the weathering effect. Rock fragments detach from the mountainside and deposit at the base, creating a 40-degree slope that has a tendency to slide. Little, if any, vegetation grows here. The rock slopes on this hike open up incredible views of a mountain called Harkening Hill.

Fallingwater Cascades Trail is part of the Peaks of Otter Trail System. About 1 mile into the hike, a trail off the loop to the right leads 40 yards up to a parking area for Flat Top Trail, a 4.5-mile trail connecting you to the picnic area at Peaks of Otter. The Peaks of Otter, a recreation area on the Parkway (between milepost 85.6 and 85.9), has a lodge, campground, and visitor center, in addition to the picnic area. You can visit the Johnson Farm, a restored farm dating back to 1852, and participate in the live demonstrations.

DIRECTIONS: **From Glasgow, take US 501 south and travel 9 miles up to the Blue Ridge Parkway at the James River. Head south on the Parkway for about 19 miles to Fallingwater Cascades Overlook (milepost 83.1) on the right.**

# four ALLEGHANY HiGHLANDS

**T**HE REGION OF VIRGINIA known as the Alleghany Highlands is home to Covington, county seat of Alleghany County, and the towns of Clifton Forge and Iron Gate. The 452-square-mile area in the James River Basin lies west of the Blue Ridge Parkway at the southern tip of the Shenandoah Valley. This part of western Virginia is over 88% forested and includes almost 135,000 acres of national forest.

For years, iron was monarch in this section of Virginia, and the economy pivoted on the vast furnaces and forges that peppered the hillsides of the Alleghany Mountains. The waters of the Jackson River, over millions of years, had worn away the mountain, exposing the colorful layers of mineral-rich shale, quartzite, sandstone, and limestone. Alleghany iron was known worldwide and was prized by blacksmiths because it was charcoal iron. Then, in the early 1900s, iron ore was discovered in the region of the Great Lakes. This Mid-Western ore was much more accessible; so by the end of World War I, the Alleghany iron industry was dead. However, the small communities remained and prospered.

The first real inhabitants of what would become Alleghany County were Shawnee, Delaware, and Mingo Indians. Terrified of Indian attack, pioneers were reluctant to settle in the region, and only the truly adventurous were intrepid enough to locate here. White settlers from east of the Blue Ridge began settling the area in the 1770s. Covington, now the county seat, recorded its earliest settlement in 1746. Covington incorporated in 1880, and Clifton incorporated in 1884.

In the 1800s, the area grew and prospered around the iron industry and the railroad. Colonel John Jordan of Lexington operated several iron furnaces and was responsible for the building of a road across North Mountain between Lexington and Clifton Forge. The road, a monumental undertaking, was necessary for wagon access to the furnaces. No one else thought the road could be built, but the colorful colonel undertook the project and saw it to completion. There is an old abandoned cemetery on the crest of North Mountain that contains the graves of

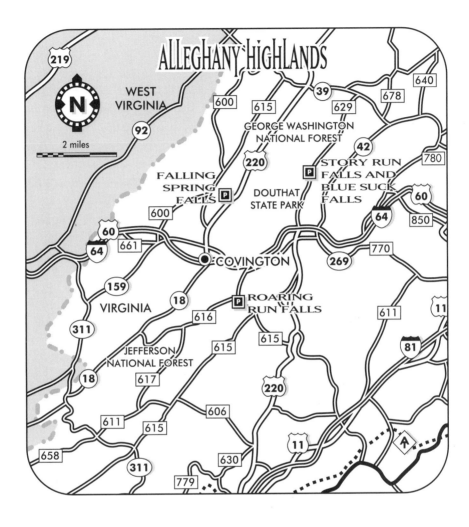

workers who died during the grueling construction of what became known as the Midland Trail.

The railroad was as important to the development of the area's iron industry. Without a link to the western waters of the Ohio and Mississippi rivers, the coal and iron of the region could never have helped fuel the Industrial Revolution. The Chesapeake and Ohio Railway (C&O) provided Virginia's connection to these western waterways. The C&O, an innovator in steam locomotives, is best known for its long coal trains. However, the railroad also claimed some of the most famous passenger trains in American railroad history–trains such as the George Washington and the Fast Flying Virginian. And legends about the C&O abound. Who has not heard the famous story of John Henry, the steel driver who beat a steam drill in a race at Big Bend Tunnel in 1872?

In 1882, the C&O opened a new depot at Clifton Forge, and the little town became an important junction for the railroad. The railroad became the principal industry of the area and the company purchased much of the property thereabouts. Today, you can visit the C&O Historical Society's Archives in Clifton Forge, which preserves and interprets the history of this railway. Railroad enthusiasts will find a visit here most rewarding. The Archives are located in the historic downtown area across from the Amtrak passenger station.

In keeping with a rich history, the Alleghany Highlands has many landmarks to entice the visitor. Follow Jordan's original Midland Trail to Humpback Bridge, the only surviving trussed arch in America. This covered bridge, a Virginia Historic Landmark used in the 1800s, is surrounded by its own five-acre wayside park—a very popular spot for picnicking. Other area landmarks on the National Register of Historic Places include the Clifton Forge Post Office (built in 1910) and the Alleghany County Court House in Covington (built in 1911).

In Clifton Forge, cultural interests include the Alleghany Highlands Arts and Crafts Center and the Stonewall Theatre. The Center has two exhibit halls and a sales room for regional fine arts and hand-crafted products. In October, the town's Shrine Club sponsors the Fall Foliage Festival, an annual celebration of nature's spectacle of color. Festival booths lining the north side of Ridgeway Street host artisans, craftspeople, antique dealers, and flea-market vendors.

In the nearby towns of Hot Springs and Warm Springs, there are natural rock pools with 98.6° F mineral waters famed for their curative properties. At Warm Springs, the baths are housed in their original eighteenth- and nineteenth-century structures and are open from mid-April until October. Hot Springs is home of the Homestead, another National Historic Landmark and a five-star resort that the same family has owned for more than 100 years.

As you might expect, though, we find nature's bounties to be the most remarkable attributes of the Alleghany Highlands. Among them are the lush George Washington and Jefferson National Forest, the Gathright Wildlife Management Area, which includes 2,530-acre Lake Moomaw, and Douthat State Park. The North Mountain Trail in the James River District of George Washington National Forest provides some excellent hiking opportunities. This path follows the ridge of North Mountain, and rocky outcroppings along the way make great places to take in the endless panoramas of the James River Valley.

# STONY RUN FALLS AND BLUE SUCK FALLS

[ 8.8-MILE LOOP, MODERATE ]

Stony Run Falls and Blue Suck Falls are located in Douthat State Park, established in 1936 as one of the first six state parks in Virginia. The Civilian Conservation Corps (CCC) left a mark of fine Depression-era landscaping, stone masonry, and wood craftsmanship throughout the park. Douthat State Park is recognized as a National Historic District. While the waterfalls won't knock your socks off, the state park is very impressive.

Douthat lies between two mountain ridges in the Alleghany Highlands and covers close to 4,500 acres. Wilson Creek runs through the park, north-to-south, and parallels VA 629. A dam, built by the CCC, impounds the 50-acre Douthat Lake; and the list of facilities is long: a store, an amphitheater, a restaurant, three campgrounds, thirty cabins, two lodges, a boat ramp, and boat and bike rentals. You can lunch under one of three picnic shelters, swim at designated beaches, fish from the creek or the lake, mountain bike, and of course, hike.

Douthat State Park offers more miles of hiking trails (over 40 miles) than any state park in Virginia. This waterfall loop consists of four trails: Stony Run Trail (orange blazes, 4.5 miles), Tuscarora Overlook Trail (yellow blazes, 0.8 mile), Blue Suck Falls Trail (blue blazes, 2.8 miles), and Tobacco House Ridge Trail (yellow blazes, 0.8 mile).

Beginning at the trailhead for Stony Run Trail, you'll climb gradually for 2.5 miles, gaining 300 feet in elevation, to Stony Run Falls. At a sharp switchback (mile 1.7), follow the short side trail to the falls. The ascent continues as you scale Middle Mountain on several switchbacks. Once on Tuscarora Overlook Trail, you'll come to a grassy clearing and a restored CCC "firewatch" cabin. This maintained overlook affords the most beautiful view in the park. Look west down into the basin of Wilson Creek and across toward the distant Beard's Mountain on the park's east boundary. Blue Suck Trail leads you to another superb view called Lookout Rock (2,560 feet), and then descends on switchbacks through a hollow along Blue Suck Run to cross the base of Blue Suck Falls at 7.5 miles. Don't miss the right onto Tobacco House Ridge Trail, which takes you to White Oak Campground (loop C).

*Note:* The loop trail crosses Stony Run and Blue Suck Run several times–with no bridges–so wear appropriate shoes. Many trails intersect the loop trail; watch the colored blazes carefully. Maps are available at each trailhead sign and at the park office.

Both Stony Run Falls and Blue Suck Falls are located on runs of the same names. They originate on Middle Mountain, the highest peak in the park. Stony Run and Blue Suck Run flow into Wilson Creek below Douthat Lake. The narrow waterfalls both drop about 50 feet, but Blue Suck Falls has three distinct cascades. Try to visit these creeks after a good rain (usually spring and early summer). There are practically no falls if these runs are dry.

**DIRECTIONS: From Covington or Clifton Forge, travel east on Interstate 64 to Exit 27 and head north on County Road 629 (Douthat Road), which runs through the park. The park office is on the right after 7 miles. The parking area for Stony Run Falls is 0.5 mile back down CR 629 on the right. The trailhead is in the center of the parking area. There are daily parking fees. To avoid hiking the additional 0.5 mile along CR 629 at the end of the loop, park a second car (or have someone pick you up) at Wilson Creek trailhead in White Oak Campground (loop C), directly across from the park office.**

# FALLING SPRING FALLS

$\left[\text{No hike necessary}\right]$

"The only remarkable cascade in this country is that of the Falling Spring in Augusta. It is a water of the James River where it is called Jackson's River. It falls over a rock about 200 feet into the valley below, and while not as wide as Niagara, it is again half as high." So wrote Thomas Jefferson in his 1778 *Notes on Virginia*. A trip to Falling Spring Falls is hard to resist after such an extraordinary endorsement from a famous visitor.

Falling Spring Falls is located about one hour west of Lexington. There are two pulloffs. The first is an overlook; the second, a small parking area with a sidewalk connecting to the overlook. The view is excellent. The creek dives off the bluff—literally leaping just as the sign in the parking area describes. The first free fall is about 70 feet, then the creek cascades for another 100 feet or so. From the overlook, you can watch the creek disappear into the valley of Falling Spring.

Falling Spring Falls originates on 60 privately owned acres that once comprised the world's largest watercress farm. The spring is fed from several underground springs—warm and cold—in separate caves. The combination creates a stream temperature that averages 65.6° F.

In the corner of the parking area to the left of the sign, an undeveloped trail (with no railings) awaits the adventurous hiker. Although we do not recommend

*Falling Spring Falls*

scrambling down this path, the executive director of the Alleghany Chamber of Commerce said a film crew made it to the bottom with a bulky movie camera and a tripod.

Across the road from the waterfall, a bronze plaque affixed to a boulder honors an American Indian fighter and courier who saved Fort Lee from the Indians in the late 1700s. The gun powder ran out; the only chance for protecting the fort was a perilous journey to resupply at Camp Union, a round-trip of three days and 240 miles past enemy forces and through fierce wilderness.

The hero who volunteered when no one else would take the ride was actually a heroine, named Ann Bailey, often referred to as Mad Ann. Her famed horse was a black pony called Liverpool. The plaque was a project of the local chapter of the Daughters of the American Revolution.

DIRECTIONS: **From Covington at Exit 16 on Interstate 64, go north on US 220. (Don't turn right onto County Road 687 for the town of Falling Spring.) After about**

9 miles, look for the brown sign that reads "Falling Spring Gorge Lookout 1,000 feet". Pull into the parking area on the left.

# ROARING RUN FALLS

[1.4-MILE LOOP, MODERATE]

Roaring Run Falls is part of a recreation area in Jefferson National Forest (elevation 1,200 feet). Hiking trails lead to the 30-foot waterfall and the ruins of an 1838 iron furnace, and there is year-round fishing in the lakes, river, and streams.

In the mid-1980s, Roaring Run Trail was designated a National Recreation Trail, meaning top priority is given to maintaining scenic quality and making trail repairs. In the early 1990s, the Forest Service did much-needed rockwork, and new tables improved the picnic area. Also, work was done to make Roaring Run Falls Trail easier and safer. In the future, a parking fee may be implemented to maintain the recreation area, as well as the quality of the trail.

Roaring Run Trail begins with a history lesson. Hike through the picnic area (fork right) and take the bridge across Roaring Run Creek to the remains of an old iron furnace. Roaring Run Iron Furnace, which operated in the nineteenth century, is on the National Register of Historic Places. A pamphlet put out by the New Castle Ranger District describes it as a "standing pre-Civil War iron ore furnace, used for making iron ingots, stoves, and other iron products for the building of America."

Interpretive boards detail how the furnace worked, explaining the role Roaring Run Creek played. In short, the creek drove the wheel, which powered the bellows that forced air into the furnace, making it burn hotter and thus melt the iron.

Walk behind the furnace, pick up the trail, and climb through a dense forest of white pine, hemlock, and birch to the high point (1,520 feet) of the hike. Be sure to take the left fork. A stone balcony affords a view of a distant cascade on Roaring Run before the descent to the creek and a trail junction. The waterfall is 150 yards straight ahead.

Roaring Run Falls, a striking 30-foot waterfall, splashes and slides down a steep, rocky drop surrounded by large conifers and birch trees. After the falls, Roaring Run Creek races through the gap in a series of shallow cascades and rapids on its way to the James River via Craig's Creek.

Finish the loop by following the course of the creek, zigzagging back and forth across it using three bridges. Back at the picnic area, you can spread out a feast on one of the tables right beside Roaring Run Creek.

*Roaring Run Falls*

Roaring Run Creek isn't a clear mountain stream. In fact, the headwaters are not in the mountains. The unusual white-green color of the water is a result of the creek's origin in limestone country, situated on private farmland in an area called Rich Patch in Alleghany County. We have never seen water this color before and found it beautiful.

The creek is stocked with trout and offers fishing at the lower end. The upper end has special native trout fishing rules that must be observed to maintain a viable population for future generations. The district ranger told us, "Opening day [in April] is a circus. There are usually about 300 cars in the parking lot. It is not quality fishing, but you can catch a trout." We recommend avoiding this waterfall hike during the beginning of trout season.

DIRECTIONS: **From Clifton Forge, take US 220 south through Iron Gate and toward Eagle Rock. After about 12 miles, turn right onto County Road 615 and travel 5.5 miles; then turn right onto County Road 621. After 1 mile up CR 621, take the 0.2-mile entrance road for Roaring Run Furnace on the left. This road ends at a parking area, and the trailhead begins at the upper end.**

# NORTH CAROLINA WATERFALLS

SECTION *three*

# five HANGING ROCK STATE PARK

**H**ANGING ROCK STATE PARK lies in one of the
easternmost mountain ranges in North Carolina, the Sauratown Mountains.
The range takes its name from the Saura Indians, who were early inhabitants of the
region. Archaeological evidence indicates that there was a large Saura village near
the confluence of Town Fork Creek and the Dan River.

Locally known as the mountains away from the mountains, the Sauratown
Mountains stand apart from their western neighbors, the Blue Ridge Mountains. The
Sauratown Mountains are stunning, rising abruptly above the adjacent terrain, which
averages only 800 feet. Moore's Knob, at 2,579 feet, is the highest point in the park.

Hanging Rock State Park, as you might guess, has a unique geological feature, the prominent outcrop of rock for which it was named. The quartzite compo-
nent of the range is largely responsible for Hanging Rock and other similar peaks.
Over millions of years, this erosion-resistant mineral has produced many impressive
ridges and knobs called quartz monadnocks. Other rocky precipices, which overlook
the Piedmont and the Dan River Valley, have descriptive names such as Indian Face,
Wolf Rock, Devil's Chimney, and Balanced Rock.

Over 300 species of flora have been identified in Hanging Rock State
Park. The forests consist primarily of oak and pine, plus a mix of hickory, maple,
tulip, and dogwood trees. Other vegetation includes rhododendron, laurel, azalea,
galax, a large variety of ferns, and flowering plants such as lady's slipper and fire
pink. The exposed rock supports moss and lichen.

Gray foxes, skunks, bats, rabbits, raccoons, and white-tailed deer are
among the mammals that call Hanging Rock home. Reptiles and amphibians
include frogs, lizards, and snakes–plus the state's only population of the Wehrler's
salamander. The park's lake is primarily stocked with two types of fish, bass and
bream. And birdsongs, by performers such as the warbler, sparrow, and wood
thrush, are most noticeable in the late spring and early summer.

On April 20, 1936, Hanging Rock State Park was established with a dona-
tion to the state of 3,096 acres by the Winston-Salem Foundation and the Stokes
County Committee for Hanging Rock. As recently as 2000, land has been added to

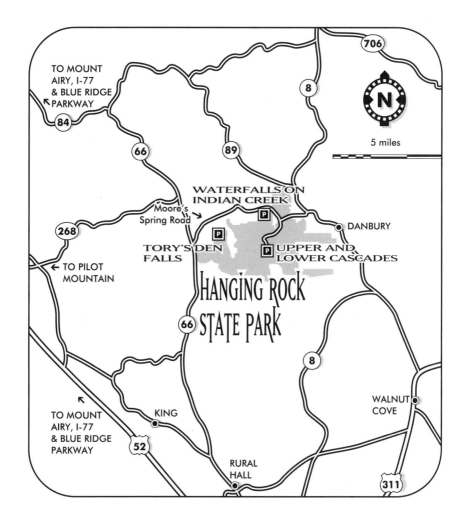

the park for a total of 6,921 acres. The Civilian Conservation Corps (CCC) is responsible for most of the construction in the park that occurred between 1935 and 1942, including a dam, a 12-acre lake, a picnic area, the park road, and several hiking trails.

Hanging Rock State Park is open year-round (closed on Christmas) and has a first-come, first-served campground with nonelectric tent and trailer sites. Each site has a grill, table, and tent pad. Bathhouses are located nearby. You'll need reservations for the group sites, which have pit toilets and water, as well as for the rustic vacation cabins, which sleep six people. The park also has two picnic areas with tables, fireplaces, grills, and rest rooms.

At the lake, although private boats are not allowed, rowboats and canoes can be rented from the boathouse during the summer. There is a protected swimming area with a sandy beach and diving platform. Facilities include a rest room, a snack bar, and a lounge area with a magnificent view.

On the Dan River, there is a boat ramp just north of the park's main entrance. The Dan River is ideal for canoeing and tubing, and anglers can spend a day trying their luck with smallmouth bass and catfish. A state fishing license is required.

For experienced rock climbers, Cook's Wall and Moore's Wall provide a series of cliffs up to 400 feet in height. All other areas are closed to climbing. Visitors must register prior to climbing and use proper equipment and safety techniques.

The park has over 18 miles of trails accessible from several different trailheads. You can hike to all five of the park's waterfalls in a day—only about 3 miles. The driving distance combined between the four trailheads equals 12 miles. Stop in at the park's visitor center (built in 1996) for maps and information. It houses an exhibit hall where you can learn more about the park's natural and cultural history through hands-on displays and videos.

To locate Hanging Rock State Park, find Danbury on your road map—north of Winston-Salem on US 52, or from the Blue Ridge Parkway at milepost 215.8 via NC 89 through Mount Airy. Travel about 2 miles north on Danbury on NC 89 and take a left onto Hanging Rock Road (County Road 2015). Continue another 2 miles to reach the park entrance.

# UPPER CASCADES

[0.6 MILE ROUND-TRIP, EASY]

Upper Cascades is the most accessible waterfall in Hanging Rock State Park— via a wide gravel roadbed. (*Note:* A paved path branches off from Upper Cascades Trail providing handicapped access to the Rock Garden Area.) The trail to Upper Cascades is one of the hikes that rangers often use for weekly summer interpretive programs. Waterfall hikes can also be set up by request for school, church, and other groups.

On the way to the falls, there is a superb mountain view from an outcrop of rock that overlooks Cascades Creek. The trail continues down to an elaborate wooden deck with three levels. Steps lead down from the platform to the edge of the creek. This gorge, like many steep ravines, escaped much of the logging in the 1930s.

Some of the oldest trees in the park, including giant hemlocks, can be seen below Upper Cascades.

The near-vertical Upper Cascades flows over a rocky drop, which is 10 feet wide and 35 feet high. After sliding into a small pool below the falls, the stream squeezes through a gap between boulders and disappears. If you want to find out where the water goes, walk back out to the gravel, take a sharp left, and go down a steep, 30-foot grade to a ledge.

Downstream from the falls, after a series of short drops, Cascades Creek heads for Lower Cascades, which must be accessed separately, and eventually flows into the Dan River. Upstream from the falls, a dam (built in 1938) on Cascades Creek impounds the 12-acre recreational lake.

DIRECTIONS: **From the park entrance, travel 1.7 miles on the main road and turn left at the sign that indicates Hanging Rock Trail. There is a large parking area with the trailhead, marked with a wooden sign, at the lower end.**

# LOWER CASCADES

$$\left[\text{0.6 MILE ROUND-TRIP, Easy}\right]$$

Lower Cascades is the tallest and most spectacular waterfall in Hanging Rock State Park. It is on Cascades Creek, roughly 2 miles downstream of Upper Cascades. A series of 30-foot drops combine for a total drop of 120 feet.

The waterfall is at the northern boundary of the park in a 91-acre section between Hall Road and Moore's Spring Road. This land became part of Hanging Rock in 1974 when it was bought from a local medical doctor, Spotswood Taylor, who owned several pieces of property adjacent to the park.

The snack bar at the lake sells postcards of Lower Cascades. The text on the back states that a Moravian botanist, Lewis David von Schweinitz, discovered the falls. Known as the father of American mycology, Schweinitz also discovered approximately 1,500 species of plants near Hanging Rock and in the surrounding area.

The trail to Lower Cascades is a wide gravel roadbed leading you to the edge of a huge cliff where you stand 100 feet above the gorge. The waterfall is almost directly beneath you. Please use caution in this area and do not venture too close to the rocky edge.

North of the falls, on Moore's Spring Road, resorts developed at the turn of the twentieth century to take advantage of two mineral springs. Until the late

*Lower Cascades*

1920s, Piedmont Springs and Moore's Springs were popular destinations for those seeking the natural spring water.

DIRECTIONS: **From the park entrance, leave the park and turn left on Moore's Spring Road. Take another left after 0.3 mile onto Hall Road. Go 0.4 mile to the parking area for Lower Cascades on the right. The trailhead is at the upper end of the parking area and is marked with a brown sign.**

# WATERFALLS
# ON INDIAN CREEK

**HIDDEN FALLS:** [0.8 MILE ROUND-TRIP, EASY]

**WINDOW FALLS:** [1.2 MILES ROUND-TRIP, MODERATE]

Hidden Falls and Window Falls are on Indian Creek Trail, part of the state's Mountains-to-Sea Trail. You can continue past the waterfalls, following the white blazes, for 3 miles along and across Indian Creek to the Dan River.

For a biathalon of sorts (hike and paddle!), arrange for a canoe to meet you at the parking area on the Dan River parking, accessed from County Road 1487, and a shuttle car to be parked at the public boat ramp at Hemlock Golf Course. Hike the 3.7-mile Indian Creek Trail and paddle the 12.9-mile stretch of the Dan River. Be sure to stop along the river at Moratock County Park and visit the Giant Fireplace, an iron smelting furnace built in 1843.

To begin the hike, walk the wide path through the picnic area and gradually descend to a fork (right). This short spur leads to Hidden Falls. After returning to the main trail and passing good views of Hanging Rock, the recently renovated (2002) trail continues to Window Falls.

Hidden Falls is nestled in a cove thick with rhododendron. Indian Creek flows over two short ledges, first a free fall, then a sliding section, to form this 15-foot waterfall. Window Falls is a scant curtain of water that spills over an undercut ledge and splatters on the rock below. You can walk backstage, behind the 20-foot curtain, and only get slightly wet. The waterfall is named for the natural window in the quartzite rock just upstream. Look through the hole and discover. . . well, guess we shouldn't give everything away!

DIRECTIONS: **From the park entrance, follow the directions to the large parking lot (see directions under Upper Cascades). The trailhead is marked by a sign at the upper end.**

# TORY'S DEN FALLS

[ 0.6 MILE ROUND-TRIP, MODERATE ]

Tory's Den Falls was named for a Revolutionary War legend about the 30-foot-deep cave near the waterfall. As with many legends, the story changes with the storyteller, but all the old tales involving Tory's Den describe the cave as a refuge for loyalists.

We like to share the story about C. Jack Martin's daughter. Martin was a member of the Whig party who lived about 15 miles from the cave during this era. His daughter was captured by the Tories, held for ransom, and hidden in the cave. Whether she was rescued because smoke was seen coming from the cave or a piece of material was found from her torn petticoat, the story has a happy ending.

From Tory's Den Trail, you can visit the cave and the waterfall. Follow the recently renovated (2002) narrow path, which is marked with plastic blue dots that

*Tory's Den Falls*

are tacked onto trees. You will come to a sign that indicates Tory's Den is to the right (descend 100 yards to the cave) and Tory's Den Falls is to the left (about 25 yards). The trail leads down steps to the rim of the gorge.

Tory's Den Falls is a delicate waterfall. A tiny creek spills over a series of rock terraces. The current is only five feet wide at the precipice, but then it divides and falls, and divides and falls again, getting wider with each drop. From where you stand, on the edge of a cliff opposite the main portion of the waterfall, you can see about 30 feet of Tory's Den Falls. Small trees and holly bushes are pushing up between rocks around the falls. The creek continues to drop on its way down the valley to the Dan River.

DIRECTIONS: **From the park entrance, leave the park and then turn left on Moore's Spring Road. Take another left after 0.3 mile onto Hall Road. Travel 2.4 miles to Mickey Road and turn left. After 0.4 mile turn onto Charlie Young Road and proceed 0.5 mile to a parking lot. The trailhead is marked with a wooden sign.**

# _six_ STONE MOUNTAIN STATE PARK

**S** TONE MOUNTAIN STATE PARK is located just
off the Blue Ridge Parkway in the quiet counties of Wilkes and Alleghany,
which are more oriented to serving anglers, hunters, and laid-back farmers than
tourists. The park, established in 1969, is home to the largest plutonic monadnock in
the state. _The New Columbia Encyclopedia,_ describes a monadnock as "an isolated
mountain remnant standing above the general level of the land because of its greater
resistance to erosion." Stone Mountain, a massive oval-shaped dome, rises 600 feet
above the surrounding valley, its base stretching a lengthy 4 miles in circumference.
Stone Mountain's elevation is 2,305 feet; its age, 360 million years.

There are countless adventures to be had at Stone Mountain State Park.
The spectacular terrain makes the park an appropriate place for a rewarding wilderness experience. No matter what your sport, Stone Mountain can help you enjoy
solitude in the woods. Even during the hectic summer season between Memorial
Day and Labor Day, the park offers some opportunities for escape.

One of the outdoor pursuits to be enjoyed in the park is rock climbing.
The granite exposures of Stone Mountain provide a plethora of explored and unex-
plored routes—some of the best friction climbing in the country. During many
months of the year, climbers can find solitude on the rock faces in the park—a rarity
in the South. You will need to check with the park office, on the right as you enter the
park, to find out where climbing is permitted.

For anglers interested in the elusive trout, there are over 17 miles of designated trout waters in the park. The native brook trout can sometimes be hooked at
higher elevations; and at the lower elevations, streams are regularly stocked with
rainbow and brown trout. The East Prong of the Roaring River, Bullhead Creek,
Rich Mountain Creek, Garden Creek, Widow Creek, and Big Sandy Creek are some
of the streams where anglers can try their luck. Check with the park office for current
rules, regulations, and fees.

Stone Mountain provides a family campground on two loop roads. All
of the sites are relatively close to rest rooms, washrooms, and drinking water.

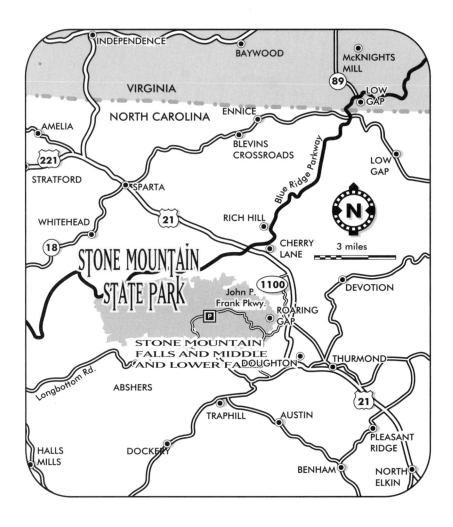

Campsites are equipped with grills and picnic tables, with your choice of wooded or meadow sites. Individual sites are filled on a first-come, first-serve basis; group sites (reservations needed) and backpacking sites (permit required) are also available. Fees are charged for all sites—individual, group, and backpacking. Stop at the park office to find out about the camping facilities.

Besides the intriguing rock faces, beautiful streams, and camping opportunities, Stone Mountain State Park has some interesting historic sites. The Hutchinson Homestead, at the base of Stone Mountain, reminds us of the distinctive cabins built by the first settlers of the area during the mid-nineteenth century. The site was restored in 1998 and is open to the public (Thursday through Sunday, from March through October). Along with the cabin, you'll find a barn, blacksmith shop, corncrib, and meat house.

Jim Hutchinson turned loose domesticated goats in the 1940s, and some of their descendants resided under the ledge near the Great Arch until the early 1990s. These surefooted feral goats would parade along the exposed ridge of Stone Mountain and could be seen on the south face. However, there haven't been goats on the mountain for years.

Stop in at the park office and visit the adjacent Mountain Cultural Exhibit. Displays include an old-time still, loom, and other historical artifacts. The exhibits help tell the story of early mountain life. The nearby 75-site picnic area has a short connector trail to the Stone Mountain Loop Trail.

As for the waterfalls, Stone Mountain State Park has four within its 13,747 acres. You can enjoy several waterfall hikes in addition to climbing, fishing, and camping. To reach the state park from the Blue Ridge Parkway, exit at milepost 229.7 and head east on US 21 towards Elkin. Travel 3 miles to Roaring Gap and turn right on Oklahoma Road. It is then 3 miles to the park. Be aware that there are no signs from this direction.

# STONE MOUNTAIN FALLS
[4-MILE LOOP, STRENUOUS]

R. Phillip Hanes, who donated over 1,000 acres to Stone Mountain State Park, saw some trash go over Stone Mountain Falls while he was on a picnic. In order to protect the falls, he decided to purchase them. The tract, which included the falls, was part of the first piece of land that Hanes bought in the area, but it was the last piece of land that he donated. Stone Mountain Falls became part of the park in 1986.

The name of this waterfall shouldn't be a surprise, but it wasn't always Stone Mountain Falls. Old maps reveal other names, including Beauty Falls and Deer Falls. Here is a strange story about the latter.

Sometimes deer who try to drink from Big Sandy Creek slip and crash over the falls to their death. Early residents saw opportunity instead of misfortune. Families were assigned different mornings to claim any deer at the base of the falls. Although a ranger assured us that the park doesn't lose too many deer in this manner, one lay at the edge of the pool on our visit.

Stone Mountain Loop Trail is your ticket to Stone Mountain View, Stone Mountain Falls, and the summit of Stone Mountain. The loop takes you through an open meadow and past the south face of the mountain. After entering the woods, you will hike a ridge to the falls. The last part of the trail takes you across the dome and down the other side to the parking area.

Stone Mountain View, within the first 0.5 mile of the hike, is a grassy meadow at the base of the south face. A plaque describes the dome as a registered natural landmark. Spread a blanket or relax on the bench. Watch the climbers struggle up routes with names like Sufficiently Breathless and No Alternative, near where feral goats used to effortlessly traverse the exposed sloping rock.

At about mile 1.5, Stone Mountain Falls, a 200-foot sheet of falling water, slides down a near-vertical, broad granite slab. The falls are on Big Sandy Creek, which actually drops a total of 500 feet. Be sure to walk out to the pool at the base before starting the hike up the side of the waterfall.

About 300 steps make up the elaborate staircase adjacent to the falls. Built in 1991, this man-made segment of trail ascends the east shoulder of Stone Mountain—alongside the falls and all the way to the top. Before the trail was improved, hikers went from tree to tree, climbing eroded switchbacks.

Controversy arose about this improvement. It seems some people didn't think a wooden staircase was particularly attractive in the woods. The Park Service claims the construction wasn't damaging. In fact, it was quite a feat. Vegetation is now protected from the inevitable trouncing of visitor's footsteps.

You reach the summit of Stone Mountain (2,305 feet) about 2 miles into the hike, after the 0.5-mile, steep incline. On top, there are sections of bare rock, lined on the edges with pine and cedar and sparsely covered with moss and lichen. Follow the yellow blazes on the exposed rock. Look north to view the Blue Ridge and southwest to view Cedar Rock.

DIRECTIONS: **From the visitor center, follow the main road for 2.5 miles to the large, paved parking area on the left, where you will find the trailhead and rest rooms.**

# MIDDLE FALLS AND LOWER FALLS [3.4 MILES ROUND-TRIP, MODERATE]

When we headed off to visit Middle Falls and Lower Falls, our first question was "Where is the upper falls?" The answer: Upper Falls is yet another name for Stone Mountain Falls. All three waterfalls are on Big Sandy Creek. Middle Falls is about 0.5 mile downstream from Stone Mountain Falls. Lower Falls is about 0.5 mile downstream from Middle Falls.

Middle and Lower Falls are accessed from the Stone Mountain Loop Trail on a side trail—an old roadbed that crosses Big Sandy several times (you may have to wade if the water's high). To reach the trailhead, follow the Stone Mountain Loop Trail for about 1 mile to a sign indicating the side trail (blue blazes) to the right. Walk 0.2 mile to a 0.1-mile spur (right) that leads to Middle Falls. Then return and continue 0.5 mile downstream to Lower Falls, near the southern boundary of the park. If you want to combine a hike to Middle and Lower Falls with the loop to Stone Mountain Falls, figure on a total of 5.4 miles.

Middle Falls is a series of small cascades, with one section that slides about 30 feet at a 30-degree angle into a large swimming hole. Lower Falls is similar, but somewhat steeper, sliding 25 feet over a smooth dome. Big Sandy narrows beyond the shallow pool; you can jump across the creek to a rock beach covered with colorful, palm-size stones.

Many youth programs bring their kids to Stone Mountain State Park and bypass the recognized highlights—Stone Mountain Falls and the summit of Stone Mountain. Instead, they head for Lower Falls wearing old bathing suits or cutoffs. Sailing down the sliding falls is part of their organized activity. I'm surprised Lower Falls doesn't have a more suitable name—Sliding Rock or Bust Your Butt Falls—like other natural water slides in the Blue Ridge.

DIRECTIONS: **From the visitor center, travel the main road to the parking for Stone Mountain Loop Trail (see directions under Stone Mountain Falls). The trailhead is 1 mile into the loop on the right where a wooden sign indicates Middle and Lower Falls.**

# WIDOW'S CREEK FALLS

[0.2 MILE ROUND-TRIP, EASY]

We were ready for a break after hiking the strenuous Stone Mountain Loop Trail, and were pleased to discover the 30-foot Widow's Creek Falls a short distance off the road on a relatively flat trail. Many stories attempt to account for the name Widow's Creek. A friend of ours who lives in Winston-Salem explained, "At one time a string of widows lived near the creek." A ranger told me a

*Widow's Creek Falls*

tale about how at least one husband (a miner) could have died. He was panning for gold and fell off the falls while trying to retrieve the tools he'd lost in the creek.

Widow's Creek Trail, which heads out from the backcountry parking lot before the bridge, leads to six backpack sites. These sites along Widow's Creek require a 1.5- to 3-mile hike. Each primitive campsite accommodates four people and requires a permit and a small fee.

Stone Mountain State Park owns all the watershed for Widow's Creek. The headwaters for Widow's Creek are just south of the Blue Ridge Parkway. The creek is one of several in the park that make up the total of 17 miles of designated trout waters. Widow's Creek flows into the regularly stocked East Prong of Roaring River.

DIRECTIONS: **From the visitor center, follow the main road for 3.5 miles. Pull over just past the bridge on either shoulder and follow the short path to the falls.**

# seven BLOWING ROCK

**B**LOWING ROCK IS ONE of the oldest resort areas in the Appalachians–a destination resort since 1889. The town, developed in the 1880s, continues to serve summer residents and vacationers. Located at milepost 291.9, Blowing Rock is one of the few full-service communities along the Blue Ridge Parkway.

This charming village offers the highest quality shops, foregoing the typical tourist fare. The windows on Main Street reveal antiques, unique gifts, and designer clothing. To add to the shopping experience, between May and October Blowing Rock hosts its famous Art in the Park program on the village square. Highlighting over 100 exhibits, this juried show brings out the best in Southern arts and crafts.

The town's namesake, the Blowing Rock, is an enormous cliff towering thousands of feet above the John's River Gorge. The rock walls create a unique formation in which northwest winds blow upward, returning light objects to the place from which they were thrown. This mysterious phenomenon even causes snow to fall upside down. Scientific explanations aside, let's recount an Indian legend about two young lovers–a Chickasaw maiden and a Cherokee brave.

Wandering blissfully through the mountains, the two found themselves atop the Blowing Rock. The sky turned a deep blood red–a sign to the brave that his homeland was in danger. Torn between his pleading lover and his obligation to help his people, the brave leapt from the cliff to certain death. The heartbroken maiden prayed to the Great Spirit. And after many days, against a backdrop of another dark red sky, a great gust blew the brave back into her arms. Ever since, the winds at the Blowing Rock have swept upward from the gorge.

You don't have to be in love with a Cherokee brave or a Chickasaw maiden to enjoy the wonders at the Blowing Rock. Located on US 321, 1 mile south of town, this attraction is open year-round. Beyond the gift shop, a short gravel trail leads to an amazing overlook where winds blow strongly. Look southwest to sight Hawksbill Mountain and Table Rock; west to view Mount Mitchell, the highest peak in the East, and Grandfather Mountain, the highest peak in the Blue Ridge.

Blowing Rock boasts several sites that appear on the National Register of Historic Places. Take the Parkway south to visit the historic Moses H. Cone Memorial Park, located on Flat Top Mountain at milepost 294. Flat Top Manor, once the

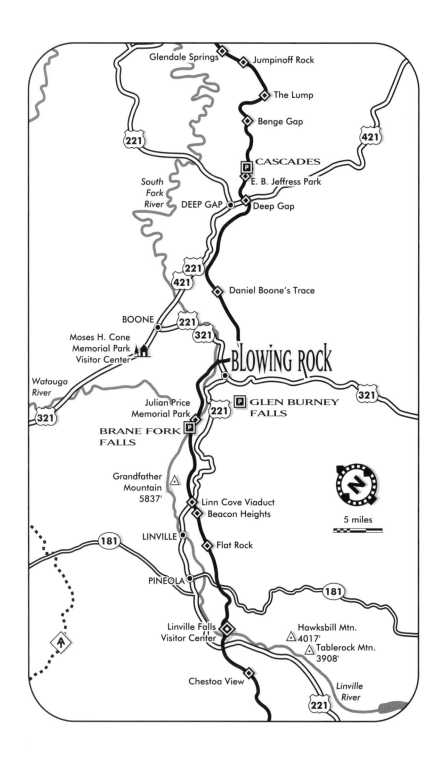

summer home (23 rooms!) of an industrialist and his family, opens in March and closes in November (no admission fee). The beautiful grounds, stretching for 3,500 acres, consist of two lakes, old apple orchards, and over 20 miles of hiking and horse trails. The impressive estate houses arts and crafts of the Southern Highlands Guild and frequent artists' demonstrations.

Other places on the National Register include the Westglow Spa, now an all-inclusive resort, which was built by portrait painter Elliot Dangerfield and remained a private home for decades; and the Green Park Inn, which has been in operation since the 1880s. A recent addition to the Natural Register in Blowing Rock is the Village Cafe.

There are two fun tourist attractions north of town on US 321/221. Tweetsie Railroad provides Western-style entertainment with food and crafts galore. Theme park rides include the 3-mile train excursion on the same steam engine used for transporting settlers around 1900. Mystery Hill Entertainment Complex provides a range of activities from a museum (circa 1903) to hands-on adventure, including the opportunity to stand inside a soap bubble.

As far as waterfalls are concerned, Blowing Rock offers something especially unique—a set of three falls practically downtown. So after enjoying Art in the Park, you can swing around the corner and take a hike. Of course, the other two waterfalls near Blowing Rock, Boone Fork and the Cascades, should not be overlooked. Located on the Blue Ridge Parkway, both waterfall hikes provide the superb scenery and excellent trail conditions for which the recreation areas along the Parkway are known.

# WATERFALLS ON THE GLEN BURNEY TRAIL

**NEW YEAR'S CREEK
CASCADES:** ·················· [0.4 MILE ROUND-TRIP, MODERATE]

**GLEN BURNEY FALLS:** ·········· [1.2 MILES ROUND-TRIP, MODERATE]

**GLEN MARY FALLS:** ·········· [1.8 MILES ROUND-TRIP, STRENUOUS]

When you ask a local for directions to a waterfall, the location is almost never downtown. Well, Glen Burney Trail is just off Main Street in Blowing Rock. From the trailhead at a town park, you can hike to three falls.

The park is actually a garden. You can walk the cedar path, which is lined with plants such as lamb's ear, borage, and wild strawberries, out to the wooden boardwalk that lies adjacent to New Year's Creek. This peaceful place is called Annie Cannon Park.

The town owned a half acre and the Cannon Family gave $100,000 to develop it into a park. Annie Ludlow Cannon, wife of J.W. Cannon of Cannon Textile Industry, taught Sunday school for years and did extensive social work, helping start the Community Club and supporting the Grandfather Home for Children. She was a true friend to the town of Blowing Rock.

Another notable friend of Blowing Rock was Emily Pruden, a school teacher who donated the land around the waterfalls to be preserved as part of the park. Around 1900, she started the Skyland Academy, a boarding school for underprivileged children. There is a marker at the south end of town (junction of US 321 business and bypass) that commemorates her benevolence.

The Glen Burney Trail is not new. Old-timers say it has been around as long as they can remember—over 100 years. You can pick up a free map of the Glen Burney Trail at the chamber of commerce.

After passing the sewage pump station and Dockside Ira's Restaurant, the trail descends into the Glen Burney Gorge. There are some ruins from the early 1920s of a nonmechanical, gravity-flow wastewater plant that served the Mayview Manor Hotel, which was torn down in 1978. For its time, the plant was extremely sensitive to the environment.

At the Cascades, a wooden bridge crosses New Year's Creek and provides a place to sit and dangle your feet over this 20-foot slide. (Don't cross on the bridge; continue downstream.) A picnic table indicates you're near Glen Burney Falls. Walk 100 yards to the observation deck at the brink and enjoy looking out over the John's River Gorge. Farther on, there is a longer side path that will take you to the bottom of Glen Burney Falls. The trail deteriorates some (steeper with switchbacks) near the last and largest waterfall, Glen Mary Falls, but a rocky outcropping affords a nice view.

DIRECTIONS: **In downtown Blowing Rock, turn off Main Street onto Laurel Lane. At the four-way stop (Wallingford Street), continue straight. Just before the bridge, turn left into Annie Cannon Park. The trailhead is just beyond the information board.**

# BOONE FORK FALLS

[ 5-MILE LOOP, STENUOUS ]

There are several books that detail this loop, but 25-foot Boone Fork Falls always gets just a mention. Even though it is a pretty cascade, the falls is upstaged by a creek with a celebrated name, a forest that was cut by one famous person and bought by another, and a trail that is one of the best along the Blue Ridge Parkway.

The falls are on Boone Fork, which was named after Daniel Boone's nephew, Jesse. He had a cabin and a small farm near the creek in the early 1800s. A huge tract of virgin chestnut, poplar, and hemlock was forested in the early 1900s by William S. Whiting, a great lumber baron. Julian Price, founder of Jefferson Standard Life, one of the nation's major insurance companies, purchased the land in the late 1930s to use as a retreat for his employees. Price was killed in an automobile crash and the land was donated to the Park Service. Boone Fork was dammed to form Price Lake, a memorial to a man who deeply loved these parts.

Julian Price Park, one of the most popular recreation areas on the Parkway, was dedicated in 1960. It consists of 4,200 acres of mountain land, ranging in elevation from 3,400 to 4,000 feet. There is a campground, picnic area, and a lake with boat rentals.

If you travel the Boone Fork Loop counterclockwise, you will first walk through an ancient lake bed where rich soil supports strawberries, blackberries, wild mustard, and pink roses. The field is great for bird-watching! Then, you will pass some rock outcroppings with several caves that provided shelter for prehistoric Indians. *Note:* About 100 yards past the unusual wooden ladder, head right and back towards the river.

The trail parallels Boone Fork. Watch for wood ducks and evidence of energetic beavers. The waterfall is 1.8 miles from the trailhead. From the guardrail, 30 feet above the creek, you can see Boone Fork rushing and falling over car-sized boulders.

After the falls, the trail heads away from Boone Fork and follows Bee Tree Creek, which you cross more than a dozen times on the way up to its headwaters. Then, there is a steep climb up a set of wooden stairs. During the last mile, you hike through open meadow, high above the two creeks, and through a section of the campground.

DIRECTIONS: Leave downtown Blowing Rock heading south on US 221. Travel 1.7 miles to an entrance for the Blue Ridge Parkway on the right. Get on the Parkway and head south (left) for 1.8 miles. Julian Price Picnic Area will be on the right at milepost 296.4. Park near the rest rooms. There is a brown sign just beyond the building directing you across Boone Fork Creek to the trailhead at the information board and map.

## CASCADES [1.2-MILE LOOP, MODERATE]

"Water . . . like liquid lace from overhead . . . dashes past to swirl and slide downward in an abandon of spray and foam ripples." The quote is from a plaque near the top of the Cascades, and it is an accurate description because the narrow, 50-foot waterfall rolls and rushes past you, rather than falling at your feet. The waters from Falls Creek are bound for the ocean at Winyoh Bay, South Carolina, after flowing into the Yadkin River, which in turn flows into the Pee Dee River.

The waterfall is not particularly spectacular, but you'll enjoy a pleasant walk on the self-guided Cascades Nature Trail. There are metal plaques along the way providing information about the flora. You will learn when flowers bloom, where certain plants live, and which trees the mountaineers used for what–knowledge you can carry with you on any waterfall hike in the Blue Ridge.

To follow the loop counterclockwise, bear right at each of the forks. The trail follows Falls Creek through a dense hardwood forest, crosses the creek on a wooden bridge near the top of the Cascades, and then heads down a well-built walkway that hugs the side of the waterfall. The upper platform is at the brink, and the lower platform is halfway down. Retrace your steps up the stairs and look for the "return trail" sign.

The Cascades is at E.B. Jeffress Park, 600 mountainous acres honoring a man who loved this land. Jeffress was chairman of the North Carolina highway department in the early 1930s. He fought hard in favor of building the proposed Blue Ridge Parkway through North Carolina.

DIRECTIONS: From downtown Blowing Rock, follow Main Street (US 321 business) north to where it intersects with US 321 bypass. Turn left (north) and travel for about 1.5 miles to the Blue Ridge Parkway. Head north on the Parkway. You will see a sign indicating that Jeffress Park is 19 miles away (at milepost 271.9). The trailhead is just beyond the rest rooms.

O**N JULY 4, 1892,** the Eseeola Inn, located in the Linville Valley, celebrated its grand opening with a spectacular gala. Except for some farms, this stately mansion with dignified guests and fancy cuisine stood alone at the foot of Grandfather Mountain.

It all began with the vision of town builder Samuel Kelsey. Ten years earlier, Kelsey founded the town of Highlands. He wanted to create another resort in this valley because he found the magic here that originally drew him to the area of present-day Highlands.

The Linville Company was organized. The president, Donald MacRae from Wilmington, presided over the first meeting and then turned the enterprise over to his son. The job called for a younger man. Donald MacRae died shortly after the hotel opened.

Several years after the hotel's grand opening, a golf course designed by Donald Ross was built. It is considered the first golf course in the mountains of North Carolina. The rest is a story of a growing and prosperous mountain resort. Linville is beautiful, quaint, and small, with little commercialism.

One of the historic buildings in Linville, the Old Hampton Store, operates the only gristmill in the area. When the Depression hit, Hampton settled with the locals, who brought in herbs, by giving them wooden coins that could be used in his community store. Stop in, browse, and don't pass up the pancake mix and corn meal. The store is open year-round.

Grandfather Mountain, the most dominant physical feature in Linville and the highest peak in the Blue Ridge, was named for the outline of a bearded man looking up towards the sky. Grandfather, whose rocky formation dates back 1.2 billion years, stands watch over this summer resort from an elevation of 5,984 feet. The Indians first called him Tanawha, "fabulous hawk or eagle," for the great birds that soar above his head. Look for his profile from NC 105 in Foscoe, about 7 miles north of Linville.

Grandfather resides in a 4,000-acre wilderness preserve that is open daily except Thanksgiving and Christmas (admission $12). At this privately owned park, you can visit the famous Mile-High Swinging Bridge, which stretches 228 feet between two peaks (or two features of Grandfather's face). Built in 1952, the bridge

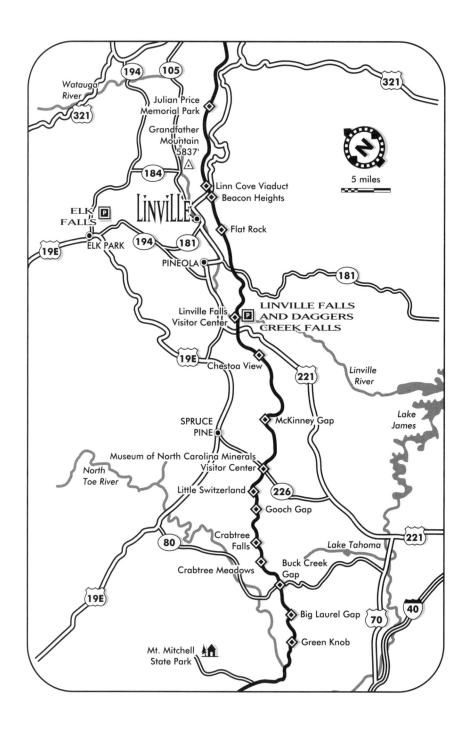

was reconstructed in 1999 and the original towers are still being used. There are seven environmental habitats, home to black bear, white-tailed deer, bald and golden eagles, and cougars. A nature museum offers over two dozen exhibits on mountain plants, wildlife, and minerals. You will also find a gift shop, restaurant, and movie theater. Hiking any of Grandfather's 11 trails is included in admission; otherwise hiking permits cost $6.

The offerings on Grandfather Mountain's calendar of events include photography workshops; musical concerts; and wildlife, birding, and geology programs. In July at Mckae Meadows near the base of Grandfather Mountain, you will find huge crowds (close to 20,000 people) enjoying a Scottish festival that goes well beyond plaids and bagpipes. The Grandfather Mountain Highland Games, considered this country's best highland games, is the annual gathering of over 100 Scottish clans.

This outdoor event begins with a traditional torch-bearing ceremony, and the following days provide visitors with the opportunity to trace their heritage back to its original clan, listen to music performances, and watch national and international championship dancing. Sporting events include tossing the sheaf and turning the caber (a young tree trunk), a traditional track and field meet, and the most difficult marathon in America, which follows a stretch of the Blue Ridge Parkway. A shop called Everything Scottish Ltd., located in Linville, can provide information about the games. Posters and flyers concerning the event are up by March.

Another attraction on Grandfather Mountain is a famous bridge not to be missed. It will take you along the side of the mountain. The Linn Cove Viaduct, a missing link of the Blue Ridge Parkway, was completed in 1983 after years of battles between the Park Service and private individuals. The environmental issue was one of the biggest concerns. Figg and Muller Engineers provided the answer by creating a design and construction method—a huge S-shaped, elevated road—that wouldn't damage the sensitive nature of the rocky Linn Cove.

The Viaduct, considered the most complicated structure of its kind, took four years to build and cost $10 million. Visit this remarkable, 1,243-footbridge at milepost 304.6. The folks at the visitor center (south end of the Viaduct) can provide more history and answer your questions.

Don't limit your visit in the Linville area to Grandfather Mountain. Head south for 7 miles on US 221 to Humpback Mountain, where two explorers, H.E. Colton and Dave Franklin, discovered a cave in the early 1800s. During the Civil War, deserting soldiers hid out here.

Today, Linville Caverns is open year-round (weekends only in the winter). You can go 200 feet below ground, where the temperature remains a constant 50 degrees. Visitors are guided on a 40-minute tour to see colorful formations such as the Frozen Waterfall and the Franciscan Monk. In addition, an underground stream supports blind trout. Hundreds of years of living without light caused many of the fish to lose their ability to see.

For a nice picnic spot, check out the Waterfalls Park near Newland (county seat), easily accessed from NC 194. There are trails along a creek and picnic tables. The two waterfalls are small but quite pretty. This recreation area is sponsored by the Newland Volunteer Fire Department.

Now, what about the waterfalls around Linville? Well, the following hikes involve more than just a parking area and a trailhead. Visiting Linville Falls, Duggers Falls, and Elk Falls will lead you to two wonderful recreation areas, complete with camping and picnicking facilities.

## LINVILLE FALLS

FALLS TRAIL: [1.6 MILES ROUND-TRIP, EASY]

GORGE TRAIL: [1.4 MILES ROUND-TRIP, STRENUOUS]

PLUNGE BASIN TRAIL: [1 MILE ROUND-TRIP, MODERATE]

Instead of several waterfalls on one trail, Linville Falls Recreation Area offers two main trails to one waterfall with a total of six different viewpoints. Hosting about 50,000 visitors annually, Linville Falls is probably the most famous waterfall on the Blue Ridge Parkway. It was designated a Natural Heritage Area in 1989.

Linville Falls is a double cascade with a vanishing act between the two falls. The upper falls is wide and gentle, pouring over several shelves for a total of 15 feet. Here, the river is lazy. Suddenly, the river disappears into a narrow channel. Out of sight, it dives 60 feet through a winding chamber before reappearing as the lower falls, a thunderous 45- foot drop, and the largest volume waterfall in the Blue Ridge. The force of this powerful river has shaped a large basin with towering cliffs. The river flows out of the pool, leaves the recreation area, and enters the Linville Gorge Wilderness.

The headwaters of the Linville River are on Grandfather Mountain, and the river flows to the Catawba Valley through one of the most rugged gorges in the country. The sheer rock walls of Linville Mountain (west) and Jonas Ridge (east) con-

*Linville Falls*

fine the water for 12 miles while it descends 2,000 feet. The difference in elevation between the rim and river is about 1,500 feet.

The Cherokees called the area Eeseeoh, which means "river of cliffs." Settlers called the river and the falls Linville to honor the explorer William Linville, who in 1766 was attacked and killed in the gorge by Indians.

In 1952, John D. Rockefeller donated the cascade tract to the Park Service. The 440-acre area offers picnic sites, a small visitor center, and a campground. Rangers conduct interpretive programs, including campfire talks and guided nature walks. An information shelter provides a large map of the trail system directing you to the Falls, Gorge, and Plunge Basin Trails.

The Falls Trail is the most popular route to view the falls. There are four overlooks along the rim of the gorge that present a variety of perspectives: First Overlook (upper falls), Chimney View (the chimney-shaped rock for which it was named and the first look at the lower falls), Gorge View (the river cutting through the mountains), and Erwins View (the spectacular gorge and a distant view of the falls).

The Gorge Trail is our favorite because it goes to the bottom, face-to-face with this magnificent waterfall. Only from the river's edge can one fully appreciate the grandeur of any gorge.

The Plunge Basin Trail, which descends about one-third of the way into the basin, is the shortest route to view the lower falls. This unusual overlook is a rocky platform jutting out from the hillside—like balcony seats at a great performance.

DIRECTIONS: **Leave Linville and head south on US 221 to Pineola. Take NC 181 heading south for about 2 miles and access the Blue Ridge Parkway on the left. Travel south to milepost 316.4 and turn left onto the 1.4-mile spur road that leads to Linville Falls.**

# DUGGERS CREEK FALLS

[0.3-MILE LOOP, EASY]

'' O ur minds, as well as our bodies, have need of the out-of-doors. Our spirits, too, need simple things, elemental things, the sun and the wind and the rain, moonlight and starlight, sunrise and mist and mossy forest trails, the perfumes of dawn and the smell of fresh-turned earth and the ancient music of wind among the trees." *—Edwin Way Teal.*

This is one of several quotes you will encounter on Duggers Creek Loop Trail, an interpretive walk into a smaller version of the Linville Gorge. Other nature writers, such as John Muir, will meet you in the woods with thoughtful words of inspiration.

From a wooden bridge, you can look upstream and view Duggers Creek Falls, one of the smallest named falls in the Blue Ridge. The creek flows through a narrow chute as it enters the tiny canyon and spills over a 10-foot ledge. The surrounding rock walls are 15 feet apart at the bridge, only 3 feet apart at the falls. Duggers Creek flows down Jonas Ridge and into the Linville River.

The trail begins in a tunnel of rhododendron that leads you down to Duggers Creek. Cross on the wooden bridge, climb two short sets of stone steps, and immediately descend from the rocky area on gradual switchbacks. After a sharp left, cross the creek again (this time on boulders), and enjoy reading the last metal plaque before returning to the parking area. *(Note:* Unfortunately, many of the signs and plaques are now damaged or missing.)

*Lower Cascades,* page 63

*Lower Catawba Falls,* page 97

*Elk Falls,* page 85

*White Oak Falls,* page 180

*Big Laurel Falls,* page 180

*Widow's Creek Falls,* page 71

*Douglas Falls,* page 108

*Toms Branch Falls,* page 176

*Whitewater Falls,* page 150

*Cullasaja River,* page 159

*Lower Cullasaja Falls,* page 159

*Falling Spring Falls,* page 54

**DIRECTIONS:** Travel to Linville Falls (see directions under Linville Falls). Leave from the sidewalk on the right at the lower end of the parking lot, and head slightly up and into the woods.

## ELK FALLS  [0.5 MILE ROUND-TRIP, EASY]

No one knows how deep the pool is at the bottom of this waterfall. The Elk River drops 85 feet over a wide, even ledge to form Elk River Falls and then crashes into a huge rock bowl that looks like an amphitheater. Divers going down with weights have not been able to fight the force pushing upward. There are several stories of bags of silver being dropped into the pool during the Civil War.

Like many place names in the mountains, the river and the falls honor the Eastern elk, a great animal that inhabited the area when wild lands stretched across the southern Appalachians. A relic of the Ice Age, the elk was the largest member (weighing 500-1,000 pounds) of the deer family and was often confused with the moose. Elk, called wapiti by the Indians, were last seen in the Blue Ridge in the early 1800s.

*Elk Falls*

There is a story about a woman who lived on the Elk River (about 9 miles from the falls) but thought she was in Kentucky. It was 1825 when Delilah Baird of Valle Crucis eloped with Johnny Holtzclaw, who was supposed to take her to his property in Kentucky. Three years passed and one day when Delilah was out gathering ginseng, she found some of her father's cattle and discovered she was only 8 miles from home. Delilah reunited with her family but then returned to her Kentucky home.

Elk Falls is located in Elk Falls Recreation Area of Pisgah National Forest. This is a wonderful place to spend a day. You can swim or fish, and there are picnic tables along the river above the falls. A few miles upstream, you'll find the Elk River Campground, where you can fall asleep to river sounds at one of the 50 oversized sites.

Don, the owner of the campground, told me that trout fishing is good there. The area is a bird sanctuary, and the pavilion has a fireplace that is set up for cooking. The campground is open year-round.

DIRECTIONS: **Leave Linville and head north on NC 181 to Newland. At the first stoplight, turn right onto NC 194 and travel 7 miles to Elk Park. About 0.2 mile north of town, turn right at the sign for the Elk River Campground; and after 0.3 mile, turn left onto Elk River Road. The campground will be on your left at 1.5 miles, and the pavement ends at about 2 miles. Follow the gravel road until it ends (another 1.5 miles) at Elk Falls Recreation Area. The trailhead is at the upper end of the parking area.**

# nine LITTLE SWITZERLAND

**L**ITTLE SWITZERLAND WAS named for its similarity to Switzerland's Jura Mountains, near the border with France. The village, filled with Swiss-style houses, literally clings to the side of a mountain. In keeping with the town's theme, the lodges and shops have names like Alpine Inn, Switzerland Inn, Edelweiss Shop, and Chalet Shopping Plaza.

Ten executives from Charlotte, searching for a cool summer retreat for their families, founded the community of Little Switzerland in 1910. They created the Switzerland Company, bought land, divided it into lots, and constructed roads and a water system.

The small mountaintop village of Little Switzerland, located at milepost 333.9, is one of the few towns that sits right on the Blue Ridge Parkway. About 0.5 mile north on the Parkway, you can drive through a 542-foot Little Switzerland Tunnel, the first in a series of 25 tunnels on the Parkway before Cherokee, North Carolina.

Although Little Switzerland's winters can't compare to those in the Alps, you can still have some fun when it snows. When the Parkway is closed to traffic, the stretch north to Linville Falls offers some of the best sledding and cross-country skiing in western North Carolina.

Geneva Hall, in the center of Little Switzerland, is the headquarters for many community happenings. The facility hosts artisans, lecturers, and musicians. Activities include everything from square dances to bridge tournaments. You will find a list of events at the post office. Take time to talk to the area's friendliest postmaster about anything pertaining to Little Switzerland.

Little Switzerland is noted for its broad panoramas–mountain after mountain after mountain, as far as the eye can see. For one of the best vistas in town, drive up to the top of Clarkson Knob (4,000 feet). The mountain, originally called Grassy Mountain, was named for Justis Harriot Clarkson, the founder of the town. Most locals still refer to the knob by its former name.

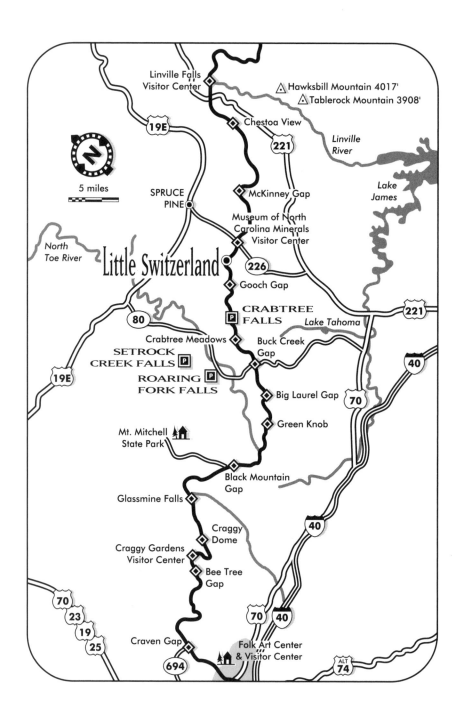

From the top, you can see Grandfather Mountain, Table Rock, Hawksbill, and the entire Black Mountain Range, including Mount Mitchell. The glitter and twinkle of distant town lights make the view sensational at night, too.

If driving up a 1.5-mile, one-lane gravel road doesn't interest you, try Woody Knob, 2 miles north of town. Some residents consider it the better view because tall vegetation is steadily proliferating on Grassy Knob.

Little Switzerland is also noted for Gillespie Gap. The Overmountain Victory National Historic Trail, which passes through Gillespie Gap (where the Parkway goes over NC 226), commemorates a historic march of the Revolutionary War. The Overmountain Men journeyed through Gillespie Gap on their way to South Carolina to fight Major Patrick Ferguson and his British army. The contest was the Battle of Kings Mountain; the date, October 1780; the outcome, a triumphant success for the Colonial forces. Every year a group of men, women, and children re-enact the march, stopping to camp at Gillespie Gap just as the Overmountain Men did over 200 years ago.

Above all else, Little Switzerland is noted for its location in one of the richest mineral and gem districts in the country–the Spruce Pine Mineral District. Commercial mining has been an important part of this area for 70 years. At one time, over 400 mines operated in the district. The minerals include emeralds, garnets, rubies, amethysts, and quartz.

The nearby town of Spruce Pine holds the annual North Carolina Mineral and Gem Festival at the Pinebridge Coliseum in late July or early August. The retail show hosts approximately 40 dealers who put out their various wares. You can choose a gemstone and a piece of jewelry, and the artisans will cut and set your stone while you wait.

To learn more about the rocks and minerals in the state, visit the Museum of North Carolina Minerals, a Parkway concession at milepost 331. The ranger is always happy to answer questions. And don't miss the Emerald Village, the number one mining attraction in North Carolina. At this museum and underground mine, you can hunt for gems, tour a recreated mining town, watch gemstones being cut, and shop for gifts and antiques. The wonderful displays and interpretive information tell about conventional methods, equipment, and about the history and heritage of miners.

Stop in at a local rock shop for directions to one of several commercial gemstone mines that are open to the public. Buy a bucket of mineral-rich ore and join the rock hounds. Just throw some dirt in your pan and wash it in the mine's flumes. If you come up empty, be assured that there are many other gems to be discovered: the waterfalls around Little Switzerland. And they may be easier to find.

# ROARING FORK FALLS

*[ 1 MILE ROUND-TRIP, Easy ]*

Roaring Fork is in the Appalachian District of Pisgah National Forest and eventually flows into the South Toe River. The trailhead is at the entrance to the Busick Work Center, a Forest Service workplace that also houses tools and equipment.

Follow the old logging road and don't be alarmed when you pass some run-down brick buildings labeled "danger" and "explosives." They held dynamite, blasting caps, drills, and jack hammers in the early 1950s when the Forest Service did their own road construction. Now that sort of work is contracted out.

*Roaring Fork Falls*

Just before crossing a bridge over the Roaring Fork, head right. Continue 100 yards upstream of the wooden bridge and reach Roaring Fork Falls, which rushes 30 feet down a narrow, zigzag slide.

DIRECTIONS: **From Little Switzerland, pick up the Parkway and head south. Travel to milepost 344.1 and exit north onto NC 80. Drive north for 2.3 miles, and just before the Mount Mitchell Golf Course, turn left onto County Road 1205, which becomes Forest Road 472 (there is a sign for FR 472 at the intersection). Take the first left (after 0.1 mile) at the sign indicating Roaring Fork Falls and Busick Work Center. The road ends at the work center. Park near the gate on the right. There is a sign that reads "Falls, 0.5."**

# SETROCK CREEK FALLS

[1.4 MILES ROUND-TRIP, EASY]

Setrock Creek Falls is located in Pisgah National Forest at the Black Mountain Recreation Area. In addition to the waterfall hike, you can ride on a bicycle trail, float down the South Toe River in an inner tube, or climb Mount Mitchell, the highest peak in the East, using the 5.6-mile Mount Mitchell Trail.

The Black Mountain Campground, at an elevation of 3,000 feet, is open between April and October. The tent and trailer sites (no hookups) have tables, fire rings, grills, and lantern posts. The group site can accommodate 50 people (reservations required). An amphitheater houses programs on weekend evenings.

On the way to Black Mountain Recreation Area, you'll pass the Y-junction of Neal's Creek Road and Forest Road 472. At one time, this was part of a state-owned wildlife refuge with a fish hatchery stocked from the South Toe River, Neal's Creek, and Curtis Creek. The Forest Service acquired the land in an exchange with the state that expanded Mount Mitchell State Park. A small stone building, formerly staffed by rangers, remains but no longer provides visitor information.

Begin this waterfall hike by walking the gravel road for about 0.4 mile to a brown Forest Service sign marking the trail on the right. Head up five stone steps and into the woods. Don't cut towards the creek too early. When the trail widens and begins a steep ascent, fork left to reach the falls.

Setrock Falls has four distinct levels, each about 10 feet high, for a total of 50 feet. The creek splashes over small boulders and then flows the short distance to the South Toe River.

DIRECTIONS: From Little Switzerland, travel to Forest Road 472 at the Mount Mitchell Golf Course (see directions under Roaring Fork Falls). FS 472 becomes gravel after 0.8 mile. There are picnic tables on the South Toe River at 1.5 miles, and the Y-junction (take right fork) is at 2 miles. Travel 0.6 mile from the fork and reach the recreation area on the right. Park at the trailhead outside of the entrance to avoid paying a fee. Walk into the campground on a cement bridge over the river and go left toward Briar Bottom (the group campsite). Hike up the gravel road to reach the trailhead.

## CRABTREE FALLS [2.5-MILE LOOP, MODERATE]

Crabtree Falls is on Crabtree Creek accessed by Crabtree Loop Trail in Crabtree Meadows. No mystery behind where this place got its name! Flowering crabtrees were once plentiful, growing wild in the fields. Unfortunately, that was in the old days when, like the many apple orchards in the area, they were maintained and cared for. Only a few scattered trees remain, but each May, they announce themselves with attractive pink blooms.

Crabtree Falls, crowned with hemlock and cloaked in rhododendron, plunges 60 feet down a wide and even rock face. The moderate volume of the creek skips lightly over the little ledges. The royal carpet that spreads out before the falls displays showy, lily-like trillium.

Crabtree Creek turned a corn mill during the first half of the 1800s. The Penlands owned the property and Billy Bradshaw managed it, hiring locals to help with crops, livestock, and most importantly, the mill. The corn mill was the main source of income; families came from surrounding valleys to bring their corn to mill. Because the creek had a small-but-fast current, Billy used a tub mill. This type of mill was designed for mountain streams and turned horizontally instead of vertically.

Crabtree Falls Loop Trail is known for its wildflowers—more than 40 species—including lady's slipper, wild orchids, and jack-in-the-pulpits. The path leads down gradual switchbacks through an oak-hickory forest. You'll cross several wet-weather springs—where salamanders flourish—before reaching the base of the falls (0.9 mile) and a large, open hollow that is covered with ferns from end to end.

Cross the creek and begin the 1.6-mile return route, which is not as steep as backtracking. As you climb the moderate switchbacks, you are rewarded with a different view of the falls. Once you reach the ridge, the trail is gentler, crossing the creek and several of its tributaries on split-log bridges. Keep left at any junction; signs will direct you back to the campground.

*Crabtree Falls*

Crabtree Meadows is a 253-acre area that lies at 3,740 feet in the shadow of the Black Mountains. Part of the Blue Ridge Parkway, its facilities include a gift shop, restaurant, gas station, amphitheater, and campground. The picnic grounds are separate—just south and across the road. Between May and October, the concessions are open and park rangers lead nature walks and give evening interpretive talks.

DIRECTIONS: **From Little Switzerland, pick up the Parkway and head south. Travel to milepost 339.5 and turn right into Crabtree Meadows, following the road to the campground information building, where you can pick up a Park Service map that gives an overview of the recreation area and trail. If the campground road is closed, you'll have to walk an additional 0.3 mile.**

# ten MARION

**M**ARION (MCDOWELL COUNTY) lies in the Catawba River Valley, 12 miles off the Blue Ridge Parkway–down the mountain, but still in the mountains. Located off a major interstate and on the edge of a national forest, Marion sits between a highway and the woods. Interstate 40 runs south of Marion, linking it westward to Asheville or eastward to Morganton much faster than small mountain roads. And, Marion is home to the office for the Grandfather Ranger District, which includes the Wilson Creek Area and the Linville Gorge Wilderness.

Much of Marion's past lies behind the walls of two historic buildings. The McDowell House and the Carson House reveal stories about the earliest settlers, the place names, and the founding of the county and the town.

The county was named for Joseph McDowell, the man who built the McDowell House, which is located on US 70 just west of the junction with US 221. McDowell's notable role in the American Revolutionary battles at Kings Mountain and Cowpens made him a local hero. His father, a fine hunter who was called Hunting John, originally settled in the valley during the 1750s.

The county was organized in March of 1893 inside the Carson House, located west of the McDowell House on US 70 and just over the Catawba River. Now on the National Register Historic Places, the house was built in 1780 by Colonel John Carson and used first as the county seat. When the courthouse was built in 1845 and the county seat was moved, the Carson House operated as an inn and stagecoach stop, receiving such distinguished guests as Sam Houston, Andrew Jackson, and Davy Crockett. Later it became a girl's school, and today is a museum.

Two months after the founding of the county, Colonel Carson presented 50 acres to create the town of Marion. The town's name came from Francis Marion, the Swamp Fox. A hero in the American Revolutionary War, Francis acquired the nickname for his sly, masterful skills in the backwoods.

Today the Carson House stands as a tribute to Southern colonial life and contains memorabilia and furniture from that time period, as well as Carson family belongings. One room in particular is given over to the historical archives and genealogical records of the people of McDowell County and western North Carolina. The house is open for tours (small fee) Wednesday through Saturday between May and October.

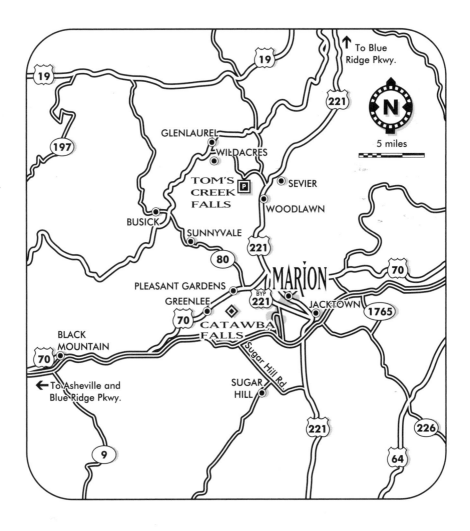

While two old homes contain much of Marion's history, one lovely mountain lake creates the center for much of Marion's recreation. Between 1916 and 1923, Duke Power Company dammed Catawba River, Paddy Creek, and Linville River. The impounded water–Lake James–took its name from James B. Duke, the founder of Duke Power Company. This 6,510-acre lake rests at an elevation of 1,200 feet and boasts over 150 miles of shoreline.

In 1987, government-appropriated funds enabled approximately 550 acres of land around Lake James to be purchased and developed into the state's newest park. To reach the entrance for Lake James State Park from Marion, travel northeast on NC 126 for about 5 miles.

Recreational activities at Lake James State Park include camping, picnicking, and water sports. The park offers primitive campsites (several with water faucets) and a bathhouse. You can picnic along the shoreline or at a table with a grill. Skiing and fishing are obvious favorites, and there is a beach, boat dock, canoe rentals, and refreshment stand. Swimming and sunbathing are popular too.

Let's not forget fishing. Anglers cast from boats as well as along the shore, and they catch bluegill, perch, walleye, catfish, bream, and crappie. The largest bass caught out of Lake James weighed over 14 pounds. Pick up some bait and rent a boat from one of the lake's landings. The park even sponsors scheduled fishing tournaments.

Marion—a regular town of average size with the usual amenities—fits the label "small town USA." The chamber has a visitor center on US 221, 1 mile from downtown. After you've visited Marion's historic homes and enjoyed a little recreation at Lake James, it's time to find the falls.

# TOM'S CREEK FALLS

$\left[\text{2 MILES ROUND-TRIP, EASY}\right]$

**W**e didn't know what to expect when visiting Tom's Creek Falls. All we had was a slip of paper from the chamber of commerce that described it as "a gentle falls in a picturesque area." We were surprised to find a 100-foot waterfall with sections of sheer drops from 5 to 30 feet and a tiny pool at the base—a perfect cold jacuzzi for two. Car-sized boulders are scattered throughout the poplar-oak forest surrounding the falls.

The falls also has a bit of history. Two stone bridge pilings remain from a narrow-gauge railroad, which was used in the 1930s to haul out timber and transport people. More recently, the fire road, called Falls Branch Road, was built to access two small tracts cut for timber sales. Later, the Forest Service developed it as a strip opening, a wildlife habitat for deer, turkey, and grouse.

As for trail directions, you will start from a gravel parking lot and when the trail forks, stay left along the creek.

DIRECTIONS: **Leave Marion heading north on US 221. You will reach the community of Woodlawn after about 7 miles. Turn left on Huskins Branch Road, just** before the Woodlawn Motel. Go 1.5 miles and park on the right in a gravel lot before a bridge.

# CATAWBA FALLS [NOT CURRENTLY ACCESSIBLE]

Access to Catawba Falls has been an issue for a long time. In 1989, the Forest Service acquired 1,031 acres on the Catawba River, including the falls, but it is surrounded by private property. You used to be able to follow an old roadbed beside a Christmas tree farm, crossing private property for 0.25 mile, to reach the national forest boundary. "No trespassing" signs were posted at the time of this writing, but there are several proposals in the works and some hope for future access to this beautiful area.

The trail–which is no longer accessible–to Catawba Falls was a popular local hike on which you followed the Catawba River the whole way. When we were there in the early 1990s, we found it fascinating to watch the river change from a flat,

*Catawba Falls*

quiet stream to a narrow mountain creek filled with small rapids and drops. The 100-foot Catawba Falls is only a few miles from the river's headwaters, which lie on the ridge to the west—the county line between McDowell and Buncombe, and the Eastern Continental Divide. There is also an upper falls, which was reached by scrambling upstream. It is much more dramatic.

To gather more information about the falls, we phoned Mary Virginia Adams, the daughter of the original owner, Colonel Daniel W. Adams. When asked if she could answer some questions about the area, she said, "We paid taxes on that land for 75 years, I think I can help you."

When we owned the land," she explained, "people were always welcome." The Baptist Assembly even had a permit to use the trail as part of their recreational program. Mary described Catawba Falls as a "340-foot cascade" and the upper falls as a "70-foot plunge." She suggested visiting in April after a spring rain. "The falls need rainfall because they are part of the headwaters."

Of interest to the history buff, there is a sawmill site and old dam site. In 1924, Colonel Adams built the old dam, as well as two powerhouses. With the help of the Catawba River, he supplied Old Fort with its first electric lights. During the last few years that the Adams family owned the land, they built the sawmill so they could sell lumber to pay the taxes on the land.

DIRECTIONS: **For information about access to this waterfall, contact the Grandfather Ranger District of Pisgah National Forest.**

# *eleven* SOUTH MOUNTAINS STATE PARK

**T**HIS STATE PARK LIES within a 100,000-acre region called the South Mountains, about 30 miles from the main ridge of the Blue Ridge Mountains. Rugged peaks and knobs rise abruptly from the Catawba River Valley. The elevations of this relatively steep terrain range from 1,200 feet along Jacob's Fork River to 3,000 feet atop Buzzard's Roost, along the park's western boundary.

The master plan for the park stresses backcountry use. In fact, of North Carolina's state parks, South Mountains has the largest emphasis on the backcountry. Relatively undeveloped, the park retains a splendid wild quality, and one of the park's highlights is the 80-foot High Shoals Falls.

While physically separate from the Blue Ridge, this area has a similar ecosystem. A biologist working the park has found over 80 species of endemic-to-endangered plants. The park is mostly forested, with oak, pine, poplar, hickory, hemlock, laurel, and rhododendron. Expect to find yellow birch and sycamore along the park's streams and plenty of wildflowers in the park's coves. There is also abundant wildlife. Over 60 species of birds common to the western Piedmont, as well as the mountains, live in the park. You might hear the black-throated green warbler or the rose-breasted grosbeak.

In the early years of the park, before annual visitation jumped to almost 100,000, common ravens nested in the ledges around High Shoals Falls. Like most large birds, ravens don't appreciate activity near their nests. So, they moved on. An active nest was seen as recently as 1991 at a set of cliffs in the park called Raven Rock.

You might see salamanders, frogs, lizards, skinks, and snakes. The white-tailed deer is prevalent, along with smaller mammals like woodchucks, chipmunks, squirrels, raccoons, and opossums. To learn more about the park's flora and fauna, check out the exhibits in the display cases near Jacob's Fork Picnic Area.

Cherokee and the Catawba Indians were the earliest human habitation of the South Mountains. The South Mountains created a buffer zone between the two tribes. Archaeological data shows no proof of Indian habitation on present-day park

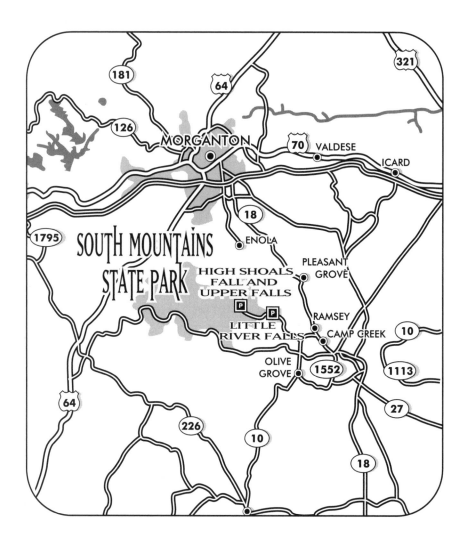

land, but Indians must have traveled through the mountains. And on the summits, the Indians probably set up temporary camps for hunting and gathering food.

Europeans (English, Welch, Scotch-Irish, and German) began arriving in the region around 1750. Farming villages were established near the Catawba and French Broad rivers. Only a few people settled in the South Mountains. Johnny Smith and his family lived on the site of the present-day park residence. Gravestones located beside the residence are the only remains of the homestead.

The South Mountains experienced a gold rush in response to an amazing discovery by wanderer Sam Martin. Local history tells the story of his visit with cobbler Bob Anderson. Martin noticed flakes of gold in the mud sealing the cracks of Anderson's log home. It was 1828, and the men headed for Brindle Creek. Martin and Anderson mined $40,000 worth of gold within a year. The gold rush, which attracted thousands of prospectors, immigrants, and slave owners, lasted only a few years. The big mining companies disappeared by the late 1830s. Although a handful of locals mined into the twentieth century, no one produced more than $500 a year after 1860.

Although the first park feasibility study was completed in the early 1940s, it took 30 years of recommendations, studies, and acquisition proposals before South Mountains State Park became a reality. The North Carolina General Assembly earmarked money for state parks in 1974. Upon receiving $1.5 million, the state was able to purchase the initial 5,779 acres used to establish the park. Employees of the Civilian Conservation Corps built roads in the 1930s that are part of the park today. Now South Mountains includes 17,615 acres and is the largest state park in North Carolina.

South Mountains does not have a developed campground, but one is planned when land becomes available. Camping is restricted to 20 backpack camping sites located in six areas throughout the park and 11 sites in a vehicle-accessible primitive camping area 0.5 mile east of the park office. Camping is first-come, first-serve and requires registration and an $8 fee. The backpack camping sites require a hike of 1.5 to 6 miles. Considered primitive camping, these grassy sites only offer fire circles, firewood, and a pit toilet. Water and all other supplies must be packed in. The vehicle-accessible sites have picnic tables.

Few state parks have a picnic facility as nice as the one here along Jacob's Fork River. Streamside and dense with trees, this picnic area offers tables, grills, modern rest rooms, and a display with a relief map of the park. Another smaller picnic area requires an easy 0.5-mile walk up to Shinny Creek. This primitive site, located in a beautiful grassy area, provides several tables, grills, a pit toilet, and additional interpretive boards.

The surface waters of South Mountains State Park consist of Jacob's Fork, Henry Fork, and Clear Creek, which drain into the watershed of the Catawba River. These steep, boulder-strewn creeks provide 14 miles of trout waters, making fishing the most popular recreational activity. While most of the streams are classified wild trout waters, a 2-mile section of Jacob's Fork offers fishing on delayed harvest trout waters.

Besides anglers, South Mountains caters to hikers, mountain bikers, and horseback riders. The park has 40 miles of trail including nature trails, bridle paths, and park roads. There are many possible loops when the trails and roads are combined. If you have a mountain bike, be sure to inquire about the 18-mile loop through the park.

South Mountains State Park is 18 miles south of Morganton. From Interstate 40, take NC 18 south for 9 miles and turn right onto County Road 1913 (Sugarloaf Road), which will end after 4 miles. Next, turn left onto Old NC 18 and travel 2.5 miles. Turn right on County Road 1901 (Ward's Gap Road) and travel 1.3 miles. Turn right on County Road 1904 and drive 3.5 miles to the park. The park is closed Christmas Day.

# HIGH SHOALS FALLS AND UPPER FALLS

[2.5-MILE LOOP, MODERATE]

High Shoals Falls, on Jacob's Fork River, is often described as the most spectacular geologic feature in South Mountains State Park. The waterfall is spectacular but so is the extensive boardwalk that leads to the observation deck at the base of the falls.

Take the High Shoals Falls Loop Trail, which begins as Headquarters Road. Signs indicate a left at the fork in Shinny Creek Picnic Area (mile 0.4). There is a large volume and variety of wildflowers along this trail in the spring. You will hike about 1 mile along Jacob's Fork before reaching the base of High Shoals Falls. The maze of well-designed wooden bridges allows passage across the boulder-strewn creek and up a steep ravine on more than 200 steps. At the viewpoint, about 20 feet from the falls, you can feel the spray from the river as it gushes over a ledge from the top of an 80-foot rock cliff, forming this spectacular, narrow falls.

The trail continues up the steps and across a small footbridge, where you can view Upper Falls, which is somewhat of a misnomer. It's just that Upper Falls isn't a waterfall in and of itself. High Shoals Falls actually drops a total of 100 feet, only 80 feet can be seen from below. The other 20 feet, labeled Upper Falls on old maps, cascades down a set of shoals with small pools in a picturesque area just upstream of the vertical drop of High Shoals Falls. Prior to the early 1990s, you had to hike a separate trail to see this small waterfall, but the park linked two trails to form High Shoals Loop Trail. They constructed a connector that climbs around the rock cliff and crosses at the top of the falls–in such a way that the visitor doesn't see any man-made structure from the base of the waterfall.

*High Shoals Falls*

An early settler to the area named Dave Bibby milled corn at the top of High Shoals Falls near the cascades of Upper Falls. He also lived close to the river. It is possible that Jacob's Fork River was named after a relative of Dave Bibby, named Jacob Bibby.

The trail continues and loops back to Jacob's Fork Picnic Area. You will leave the creek and travel through an oak-hickory forest as you descend a ridge on switchbacks. Finally, descend a gradual old roadbed back to Shinny Creek Picnic Area and on to Headquarters Road. The trail is well-signed.

You will pass the possible site of an old still about 0.5 mile before Shinny Creek Picnic Area. At one time, the area that is now South Mountains State Park was known for its moonshine. In the park, several dismantled stills are marked by rusted buckets and axed barrels. The name Shinny Creek was derived from the moonshining days.

The watershed for Jacob's Fork River is extremely pure because the headwaters are contained within park boundaries. Three major creeks, Murray Branch, Nettles Branch, and Jacob's Fork Branch, form the upper end of the river. Jacob's

Fork River, one of the first rivers in North Carolina to be considered outstanding resource water, is classified as a II (pristine with some development) on a watershed scale from I to IV. The river contains no direct pollutants and is about as clean as surface water gets (bacteria may be present, however, so drinking is not advised).

DIRECTIONS: **From the main parking area at South Mountains State Park, walk through Jacob's Fork Picnic Area and past the rest rooms to pick up Headquarters Road.**

# LITTLE RIVER FALLS

[ 4 MILES ROUND-TRIP, MODERATE ]

A ranger at South Mountains State Park had this to say about Little River Falls: "When it's in full water, it's every bit as pretty as High Shoals Falls." We agree! The Little River cascades down several tiers for a total of 100 feet. Two sections each free fall 30-40 feet.

The trail to Little River Falls is not well developed and practically bypasses the falls. A rough footpath leads off the trail and down to the base of the waterfall. The reason? South Mountains State Park only owns the upper half of the falls just above the biggest drop. They are trying to buy the land containing the remainder of the cascade and intend to complete a trail to the bottom, as well as an observation deck and viewing area.

The land east of the trail (off to the right on the way to the falls) is South Mountain Game Land–over 4,600 acres leased to the North Carolina Wildlife Resource Commission. Little River Trail ends about 1 mile after the falls at Upper CCC Trail. The nearest camping to the waterfall is Sawtooth Trail Campsites, located off Upper CCC Trail on Sawtooth Trail.

The watershed for the Little River is the east section of Horse Ridge where several branches come together. Part of the headwaters of the Little River is on timber land logged 15 years ago by Champion Paper Company. This tract is now part of the park. A good hard rain brings silt down the mountain, so the water quality of the Little River doesn't match that of Jacob's Fork River.

DIRECTIONS: **From the main parking area at South Mountains State Park, drive back towards the entrance for 0.4 mile to Cicero Branch Parking Area on the right. The trailhead is directly across the road.**

# twelve ASHEVILLE

**A**SHEVILLE, ONE OF THE BIGGEST towns in the Blue Ridge, has a population of 70,000 (county, 200,000). The *Rand McNally Places Rated Almanac* consistently rates this city as one of the best places to live among U.S. metropolitan areas with fewer than 250,000 people. That says a lot about Asheville, but here's more.

First, because of Asheville's size, you will probably want to purchase a map. Visit Malaprop's Bookstore in the middle of downtown next to the Civic Center. In addition to purchasing a map at this local hangout, you can browse through books by area authors and sip a latté while listening to local music and poetry readings.

Did you know that author Thomas Wolfe spent his childhood years in Asheville at his mother's boarding house? He recreated this house in his book *Look Homeward Angel*. The Thomas Wolfe Memorial keeps up his family's old Kentucky home just as he would have remembered it.

You haven't been to Asheville until you've visited the Biltmore Estate. George W. Vanderbilt built his 250-room mansion in 1895, patterned after the sixteenth century châteaux of the Loire Valley in France. Famous architect Richard Morris Hunt designed the house; and landscape architect Fredrick Law Olmsted, who also designed New York's Central Park, planned the grounds.

The Biltmore House provides a visit to the elegance and opulence of Victorian society. The artwork and furnishings retain their perfect condition, the extensive gardens and grounds erupt into a grand display of color in the spring, and the winery offers a look at the science and lore of wine making. Recently, the Biltmore Estate added a 213-room hotel, Inn on the Biltmore Estate, and an outdoor program called Explore Biltmore Estate, which includes horseback riding, mountain biking, hiking, and river trips.

Another of Asheville's beautiful buildings, the massive Grove Park Inn Resort and Spa, stands on the opposite side of town. William Grove had the Inn built out of local stone in 1913. The lobby is 80 feet wide and almost half as long as a football field, and the mammoth fireplaces at either end burn 12-foot logs. Like the Biltmore Estate, the feeling is one of granduer. In 2001, the Inn added a $40 million spa. The architecture and decor is in keeping with the Arts and Crafts era and sports the solid oak furnishings of that time.

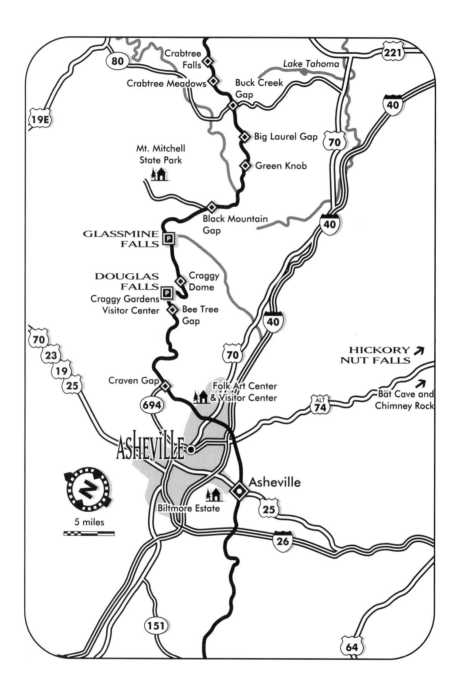

As the cultural center of western North Carolina, Asheville attracts artisans from throughout the region. Many shops display their pottery, weaving, woodworking, and handmade musical instruments. The Folk Art Center, east of town at milepost 382 on the Blue Ridge Parkway, supports a retail shop, as well as a gallery with outstanding exhibits. The Center holds special programs and demonstrations throughout the year. The Biltmore Village, located on US 25 before the entrance to the Biltmore Estate, was constructed to house the servants and workers who staffed the Biltmore House. Now many of the original buildings have been turned into shops. The New Morning Gallery is extremely well-known. They have a section devoted to arts and crafts that were made in North Carolina.

With its excellent restaurants, Asheville combines the variety of a big city with the quality and atmosphere of a small town. For breakfast downtown, try the Blue Moon Bakery (Biltmore Avenue) or Gold Hill Espresso and Fine Teas (Haywood Avenue). The Market Place (Wall Street), a longtime fixture of the downtown area, serves fabulous meals. Salsas (Patton Avenue) and Zambras (Walnut Street) are the creative works of local chef and owner Hector Diaz. He is known for his "improbable combinations" *(New York Times)*—once serving a burrito with sweet potato, eggplant, ramp onion, wild boar, and seaweed salsa. Tupelo Honey (Patton Avenue) is a newcomer to town with great Southern fare, and Savoy (Merrimon Avenue) is the place for Italian.

Asheville hosts many convivial annual events. Every July, a downtown street festival called Bele Chere attracts more than 300,000 people for three days of music, dance, crafts, and frivolity. In August, the Mountain Dance and Folk Festival, a tradition for more than 75 years, draws bluegrass musicians and big circle dancers to the Diana Wortham Theatre to compete for $2,500 in prizes. Any Saturday night in July and August, it would be worth your while to wander over to the Buncombe County Court House for Shindig-on-the-Green. This free outdoor musical event includes bluegrass, gospel, and mountain music, as well as clogging and big circle dancing.

Don't spend all your time in Asheville because the Blue Ridge Parkway, which passes on the east edge of town, will lead you to several waterfalls. Just head north, watching the mile markers, and enjoy the scenery along this famous road. In addition, make time to visit Hickory Nut Falls at Chimney Rock Park, southeast of Asheville.

# DOUGLAS FALLS

[ 6 MILES ROUND-TRIP, STRENUOUS ]

On the Douglas Falls Trail, you will discover two stands of virgin hemlock and two pretty waterfalls (the other one is Cascade Falls). The enormous trees are a definite highlight, some of which are eight feet around. This forest is enchanting! It doesn't take much imagination for the place to come alive with dancing fairies and tiny leprechauns.

The trailhead is near Craggy Gardens, a Blue Ridge Parkway recreation area that is famous for its balds, which aren't completely bare. These grassy balds support wildflowers, grasses, and other low-growing plants. The heath balds support shrubs like rhododendron, laurel, and flame azalea. Scientists don't agree on why these balds exist. Some believe the land was cleared for livestock or to attract game, others blame fire or drastic climate change.

*Douglass Falls*

Don't miss seeing the balds between mid-June and early July when the pink and purple blooms of the native rhododendron star in the most dazzling flower pageant on the Parkway. These shrubs color the slopes and peaks of the Craggies, acre after acre. In addition to the balds and rhododendron display, Craggy Gardens has gnarled trees. The beech, birch, and mountain ash have been twisted and dwarfed by the severe wind and ice storms and the short growing season at this elevation (5,500 feet).

While the trailhead is on the Blue Ridge Parkway, the majority of this white-blazed path is in the Big Ivy Area of Pisgah National Forest. For the most accurate information and directions, be sure to check with the folks at the Craggy Gardens Visitor Center, where you'll also find exhibits and a small bookstore.

DIRECTIONS: **Pick up the Blue Ridge Parkway in Asheville by first heading east on I-240 and exiting onto US 74. After about 0.5 mile on US 74, you will drive under the Parkway. Take a right and go up the ramp to access the Parkway. You will be near milepost 385. (Several signs along the route direct you to the Blue Ridge Parkway.) Travel north for about 20 miles. Craggy Gardens Visitor Center is at milepost 364.6.**

# MITCHELL FALLS

[ NOT CURRENTLY ACCESSIBLE ]

Mitchell Falls lies on private land just outside the western boundary of Mount Mitchell State Park. Even though the falls are not accessible to the public, there is a story worth telling. The 40-foot Mitchell Falls was named for Elisha Mitchell, a native of Connecticut and professor at the University of North Carolina. Mitchell fell to his death from the falls while trying to prove his claim that Mt. Mitchell was the highest peak in the East.

In June 1857, he was remeasuring the mountain because his earlier findings had been challenged. A search party led by Big Tom Wilson, a local backwoodsman, found his body in a deep pool below the falls. Elisha Mitchell is buried on his mountain near the observation tower.

Mount Mitchell and 18 peaks over 6,300 feet form the highest range in the East, the Black Mountains. They were named for the dark green color of the spruce and fir trees. For more than a billion years, wind and water rounded the towering pinnacles; the resistant igneous and metamorphic rock of Mount Mitchell endured.

In 1916, as a result of Governor Craig's efforts, the area became North Carolina's first state park. The second highest peak in the East, Mount Craig (6,647 feet), was named in his honor. Besides the most impressive view around, this 1,855-acre park has tent camping, picnic grounds, a restaurant, and a small weather station. The park has a bookstore at the interpretive center and several good hiking trails.

The exhibit hall, our favorite place at Mount Mitchell State Park, allowed us to get to know Elisha. Half the building is dedicated to sharing his story. There are photographs of Elisha, Big Tom, and Mitchell Falls. You will even find the last letter Elisha wrote to his wife before his death.

When you visit the park, it's hard not to notice the dying trees. The two dominate species, Fraser fir (found above 5,500 feet) and red spruce (found as low as 4,500 feet), are disappearing. In the last ten years, the death rate of virgin timber has been startling. Scientists believe there are several contributing factors, including harmful insects and high ozone levels. Extreme weather—winds of 100 miles per hour, ice storms and a growing season of only four months—also plays a big role.

DIRECTIONS: **Although this waterfall is not accessible, you can visit Mount Mitchell State Park. Pick up the Parkway in Asheville (see directions under Douglass Falls) and head north for about 30 miles. Turn left onto NC 128 at milepost 355.4 and travel 5 miles to the parking area near the summit. The park is closed on Christmas Day and during periods of heavy snow.**

# GLASSMINE FALLS $\left[\text{No hike necessary}\right]$

From a pulloff on the Blue Ridge Parkway (at 5,197 feet), you can look across the valley and see Glassmine Falls sliding 800 feet down Horse Range Ridge. Surprised at the height? It is hard to judge how tall a waterfall is when it's so far away.

Glassmine Falls is part of the Asheville Watershed. Rivers and creeks run down the slopes of this valley into the North Fork Reservoir, and the water is pumped to the city. So Glassmine Falls plays a part in supplying water to the people in Asheville.

Near the base of the falls is an early-1900s pit mine and cabin site. Miners once used pack animals to haul mica to Micaville and Burnsville in the Toe River Valley. It is the oldest mineral industry in the area, and a truckload of high-quality mica could bring in thousands of dollars then. Mica used to be referred to as isinglass, and people in the mountains called it glass. The waterfall got its name from the glass mine.

This is a wet-weather falls, which means it will almost disappear during periods of low water. If you can't visit Glassmine Falls after a heavy rain, try late afternoon. With the sun shining on the falls, the wet rock face looks like glass.

An observation area with a wooden bench—up the paved sidewalk and to the left—makes a nice rest stop. In addition to the view east of Glassmine Falls, look west for an incredible view of Roan Mountain. Binoculars and a camera lens with a focal length of at least 200mm will make this waterfall more fun.

DIRECTIONS: **Pick up the Parkway in Asheville (see directions under Douglas Falls) and head north for about 25 miles. Turn into the overlook for Glassmine Falls on the right at milepost 361.2.**

# HICKORY NUT FALLS

TOP: [1.5 MILES ROUND-TRIP, STRENUOUS]

BOTTOM: [1.4 MILES ROUND-TRIP, MODERATE]

Ride an elevator up 26 stories through solid granite and cross a clear-span bridge onto the famous, 315-foot monolith of Chimney Rock to start your hike to Hickory Nut Falls—a most interesting way to reach the trailhead. This is just one way to access the waterfall at the private Chimney Rock Park, where Fall Creek flows over a vertical lip on Chimney Rock Mountain, dropping an impressive 400 feet. The elevator operator will give you an introduction to the area on your ride up. Several scenes from the 1992 film *Last of the Mohicans* were filmed at the park, including the climactic fight shot at the top of the falls. Chimney Rock is located on the eastern edge of the Blue Ridge Mountains, about 25 miles southeast of Asheville.

Get a park map when you arrive and decide how to spend your day. The Skyline Trail (accessed from the top of the elevator) and the Cliff Trail lead to the top of the falls and create a loop. These trails include numerous stairways, low and narrow passages, and boardwalks that help you negotiate the rocky cliffs. You will reach vantage points with names like Exclamation Point and rock formations with names like Opera Box, Groundhog Slide, and Wildcat Trap. You can view the waterfall from Peregrine's Rest and Inspiration Point. Forest Stroll Trail takes you through beautiful hardwoods to the bottom of the falls, where Fall Creek splashes into a pool. Be sure to add this trail to your hiking plans.

Hickory Nut Falls aside, the 1,000-acre park is worth a visit for other reasons: incredible views, well-designed interpretive trails, and an informative nature center. From the top of towering Chimney Rock, you can see the Rocky Broad cutting its way through Hickory Nut Gorge, Lake Lure below, and Kings Mountain, 75 miles away. The trails have numbered stations and accompanying interpretive pamphlets to enhance your experience. At the nature center, you can learn about the birds, wildflowers, and geology of the park. One exhibit is dedicated to the history of Chimney Rock and the story of the Morse family, who have owned the park since 1902.

DIRECTIONS: **From Asheville, head east on US 74A, which will become US 64/74 after Bat Cave. You can pick up US 74A from the east side of the city at the junction of Interstate 240 and 40, at Exit 9 or 53, respectively; or get off the Blue Ridge Parkway at milepost 384.7. Chimney Rock Park is on the right after about 20 miles. After paying the entrance fee (adults, $12), you can choose from two parking areas. The park is open year-round except Thanksgiving, Christmas Day, and New Years Day. Summer hours are 8:30 a.m. to 7 p.m. (The ticket plaza closes at 5:30.)**

**B**REVARD, THE COUNTY SEAT of Transylvania County, once belonged to American Indian tribes, as did most of Appalachia. Before white traders began coming from South Carolina and parts of North Carolina, numerous Indian paths crisscrossed present-day Brevard. The first white settlers were enticed here in the middle of the eighteenth century by the rich soil and abundant game. They called it Cherokee Crossing and referred to the clearings in the forests, which the Indians burned in order to make hunting easier, as mountain prairies.

The territory that became Transylvania County was not made available for grants until after 1785, when a treaty with the Cherokee transferred the land to the government. Revolutionary soldiers received some of the grants for their service to the colony. According to George H. Smathers's book *The History of Land Titles in Western North Carolina,* one of the first land grants—50 acres on Catheys Creek, about 4 miles west of Brevard—was given to William Porter on October 11, 1783.

On February 15, 1861, a government act provided for the formation of Transylvania County from Henderson and Jackson counties. The first court session, held at the Valley Store of B.C. Lankford on May 20, 1861, established a committee of citizens to select a permanent seat of justice, to be named Brevard and to be located within 5 miles of William Probart Poor's store. (The Valley Store was later the location of Straus Elementary School, and Poor's store was located on the site of the present-day Red House.) The court also authorized paying volunteer soldiers the sum of $15. This timely decision occurred on the same day that North Carolina voted to secede from the Union. The newly formed Transylvania County found itself at war.

The county seat of Brevard, named in honor of Dr. Ephraim Brevard, was incorporated in 1868. Unfortunately, the prominent surgeon and Revolutionary colonel never laid eyes on the town that bears his name. Famous for having penned the Mecklenburg Declaration of Independence in 1775, which did not surface until long after Thomas Jefferson's declaration in 1776, Dr. Brevard helped establish Queens College in Charlotte, North Carolina. He practiced medicine and taught at the college. During the Revolution, the British captured Colonel Brevard in Charleston, where he died in prison of an unknown disease at the age of 37.

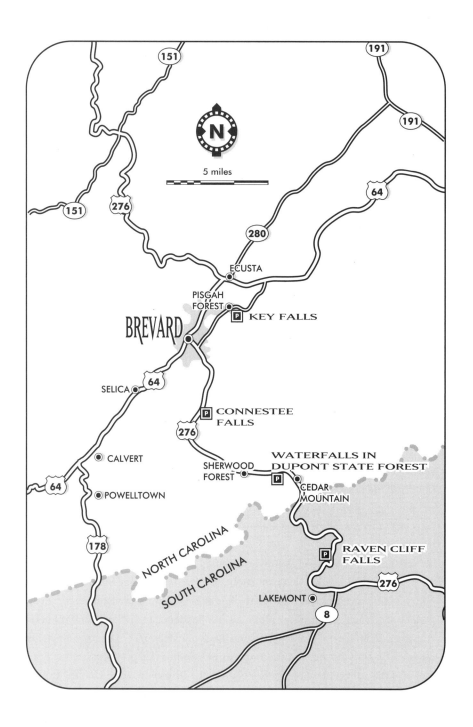

In 1985, the citizens of Brevard erected a statue in Ephraim Brevard's honor in front of the city offices on West Main Street. While many proclaim him Father of the City, others say that the town was named for all the Brevard brothers. There were seven, all heroes of the Revolution.

Like all pioneer communities, especially mountainous ones, the little town of Brevard suffered the economic woes of isolation. The few roads that existed were little more than ruts. And the one ambitious attempt to navigate a steamship on the shallow and swiftly flowing French Broad River ended in disaster.

In 1876, Colonel S.V. Pickens formed the French Broad Steamboat Company. Under the colonel's leadership, the company built the *Mountain Lily,* a sidewheel steamer capable of carrying almost 100 passengers. After completing the ship, the company determined that the river was too shallow. Workers hauled in huge loads of rocks in an attempt to alter the river's flow and make the channel deeper. The day of the launch arrived amid much fanfare and ballyhoo. The excitement reached such a pitch that Brevard declared a holiday.

The accounts of what actually happened that day vary. (1) A sudden downpour caused the *Mountain Lily* to become stranded on a sandbar before she ever made the trip. (2) The steamboat didn't clear a low bridge that her builders had not taken into consideration. (3) The ship made the round-trip from Mud Creek to Elmbend Bridge before sinking at the dock. Whatever happened, the *Mountain Lily's* maiden voyage was also her last.

Mud jammed the jetties and interfered with the river's natural flow. To add insult to injury, the taxpayers lost $43,000. The only tangible reminder of the *Mountain Lily* is Horseshoe Baptist Church, which was built with lumber from the ship; her bell was mounted in the steeple. Luckily for Transylvania County, the railroad was on its way.

In 1894, the first train came to Brevard on the Hendersonville and Brevard Railroad. By 1899, two trains ran daily between these two mountain towns. The railroad marked the beginning of an unprecedented boom for the county.

Railroads always attracted men of wealth and power. It was no different for Brevard. Industrialists who came to the area from Pennsylvania with great visions of a glorious future encouraged development of the county. These men, instrumental in Brevard's economic development, included Joseph S. Silversteen, who arrived in 1859, and J. Frances Hayes, who arrived in 1890.

A civic and community leader, Silversteen bought 140,000 acres of forestland and set up lumber mills in Rosman, just southwest of Brevard. Among

Silversteen's other ventures were the Toxaway Tanning Company, founded in 1901, and the Gloucester Lumber Company, founded in 1911.

Silvermont, Silversteen's legacy to Brevard, is a colonial revival mansion built in 1917 on eight acres of East Main Street near the business district. The Friends of Silvermont formed in 1981 to maintain the estate, which is on the National Register of Historic Places. Today the mansion hosts meetings and special functions.

J.F. Hayes supposedly came south for health reasons; but as an entrepreneur, he must have also been attracted by the lumber and other natural resources. In 1896, Hayes organized the Toxaway Company, which was responsible for building Brevard's first fine hotel, the Franklin, in 1900. Visitors enjoyed luxurious accommodations and a real bath. The Franklin was just the beginning for Hayes, who went on to build many other resorts catering to wealthy tourists.

Today, Brevard offers small-town charm and a genteel hospitality. In addition to the area's bountiful natural resources, Brevard has fine music, an outstanding theater, and several arts festivals. The Brevard Chamber Orchestra, organized in 1976, presents three concerts each year. The group includes many notable musicians from western North Carolina and also presents guest artists. Long known as the Summer Music Center of the South, the town is also home to the Brevard Music Center, recognized as one of the five major institutions of its type in the country. Each summer students come here from all over the world to study and perform with faculty and guest artists on the 120-acre campus located in the mountains on the outskirts of Brevard. Founded in 1936 by Dr. James C. Pfohl at Davidson College, the center moved to its present location in 1944.

Brevard College, a two-year institution, occupies 140 beautiful acres near the center of town. Three schools merged in 1934 to form Brevard College: Rutherford College (chartered 1853), Weaver College (chartered 1872), and Brevard Institute (chartered 1895). The majority of Brevard College graduates go on to four-year schools.

The 43-year-old Brevard Little Theater, an active local theater company, does several productions each year. Annually, the Festival of the Arts runs during the second week of July and features art shows, craft exhibits and demonstrations, and musical events.

Brevard offers great shopping–antiques, collectibles, and crafts. The White Squirrel Shoppe and the Workshop & Company at Jordan Street Center sell antiques, unique white squirrel memorabilia, local crafts, and handcrafted furniture. If you appreciate pottery, don't miss Mud Dabbers Pottery and Crafts, located 4 miles south of town on Greenville Highway (US 276). Run by the John Dodson family, the shop contains unique handcrafted creations that are irresistible.

A number of charming bed-and-breakfast establishments in the area include The Red House on West Probart Street and The Womble Inn on Main Street. Built in 1851, The Red House was Brevard's first post office as well as William Poor's store. The structure has been renovated and added to over the years, but the foundation is considered to be the oldest in town.

The Womble Inn has a homey atmosphere and rooms furnished with antiques from the eighteenth and nineteenth centuries. The innkeepers, Beth and Steve Womble, act as gracious hosts. If you would like to take a picnic on one of your waterfall hikes, Beth can provide a delectable specialty food basket.

Across the street from the Womble Inn, Oh! Susanna's serves up fresh food in a laid-back atmosphere with friendly service. We especially enjoyed the Christmas tree that adorned the dining room when we were there in February.

Brevard's snow-white squirrels, which can be seen in Franklin Park off Franklin Street and in some of the wooded neighborhoods, are not albinos. This rare species traces its roots back to a pair brought in 1949 by H.H. Mull as a gift to his niece. One account says he bought the squirrels from a ship's captain in Florida; another version says he obtained them after they escaped from an overturned carnival truck. At any rate, inevitably one of the squirrels escaped, so the family let the other one go, hoping they would find one another. They did, and today an estimated 200 white squirrels scamper around Brevard.

You can learn more about Brevard through a photographic exhibit at the Transylvania County Courthouse on the corner of Broadway and East Main. Completed in 1861 and registered as a National Historic Place, the courthouse features a square central Italianate-style tower. The Brevard/Transylvania County Chamber of Commerce, under the direction of Esther Wesley, also provides excellent information.

It is easy to see why Rand McNally recommends Brevard as an ideal retirement spot. Spend some time exploring this delightful mountain community. But ultimately, we hope that your adventures will lead you to the rivers and waterways that are hosts to the sparkling, tumbling waters for which this area is so well-known.

## Transylvania County—the Land of the Waterfalls

Transylvania County, long touted as the Land of the Waterfalls, boasts of literally hundreds of falls, cascades, shoots, and slides—every type of waterfall imaginable. The county has more waterfalls than any other in the Blue Ridge Mountains, and possibly the United States. These waterfalls can occupy devoted hikers for a long time. Sources vary, but the estimated number of significant waterfalls ranges from 250 to 500, although many of these falls are on private property.

The county's large number of waterfalls result from a variety of reasons: elevation change, rainfall, geology, and hundreds of miles of streams. Located on the Blue Ridge Escarpment, the county's highest mountains quickly give way to the Piedmont. From 6,025 feet on top of Chestnut Bald in the northwest, the terrain drops to 1,100 feet where the Toxaway River meets Lake Jocassee at the border of South Carolina. Also, the rock here is more erosion-resistant than other areas of North Carolina, and the county's average rainfall is 70–80 inches.

The French Broad, the major river in Transylvania County, flows through the Sylvan Valley to the county's eastern border. Many prominent streams empty into the French Broad, including the Davidson and Little Rivers, and Catheys and Carson Creeks. The Whitewater, Thompson, Horsepasture, and Toxaway Rivers are located at the southern end of the county. Other significant waterways in that area include Indian, Bear Wallow, Toxaway, and Rock Creeks. All of these spill into Duke Power Company's Lake Jocassee. Hundreds of other arterial streams flow throughout the county.

Many of the county's creeks have multiple waterfalls. The North Fork of the French Broad River alone has 20, and the West Fork has 19. Bear Wallow Creek sports 10 waterfalls. Jim Bob Tinsley, Transylvania County's foremost authority on waterfalls, wrote *Land of the Waterfalls,* the definitive volume on waterfalls in the area and a fascinating account of the stories behind the waterfalls. Trained as an aerial photographer in the Navy during World War II, Tinsley has chronicled the background of the Transylvania County waterfalls through his photographs and captivating tales. Some of the mills and other structures he captured on film have since collapsed or been removed.

Having grown up in Transylvania County, this retired educator, now 82 years old, knows more about the history and topography of the area than anyone. Along with being an accomplished author, Tinsley is a cowboy singer of great renown. His many achievements are honored at the Jim Bob Tinsley Museum, which opened in 1994 in Brevard.

Because of his knowledge of waterfalls and area history, Tinsley taught a popular adult education course on the subject at Brevard College. His well-recognized expertise as a photographer and historian filled the class up quickly. During the three-day course, he led students to as many as 20 waterfalls.

We had the great fortune to spend a day of waterfall hiking with Tinsley and his wife, Dottie, as our guides. And what an adventure it was! Many of the trails he led us on had been overgrown for years. We crossed over creeks, under barbed wire, and through dense laurel thickets with Jim Bob in the lead and Dottie matching him step-for-step. At Frozen Creek Falls, our expert guide pointed to the remnants of a once flourishing grist mill, which he photographed in the 1950s.

Jim Bob Tinsley's fascination with waterfalls began when he was a very young boy. Having grown up in the Land of the Waterfalls, Tinsley says that waterfalls have always been an important part of his life. For us, having discovered the joy of these falling wonders in recent years, it was indeed a privilege to have seen some of them through the eyes of "Mr. Waterfall."

There are an incredible number of waterfalls in Transylvania County, and we have divided the area into three base towns—Brevard, Pisgah Forest, and Lake Toxaway. Brevard, the county seat, sits near the center of the county; to the northeast, you'll find the quiet crossroads community of Pisgah Forest; and the southwest corner of the county hosts the quaint resort town of Lake Toxaway. You will visit some waterfalls on private property, but a third of the county is made up of Pisgah National Forest, DuPont State Forest, and Gorges State Park, where trails will take you to some of our favorites in the Land of the Waterfalls.

# KEY FALLS

$$\left[\text{0.4 MILE ROUND-TRIP, EASY}\right]$$

Would you like to take a step back in time? On the grounds of the Key Falls Inn, a small but charming cascade quietly invites you to linger at this quaint country inn and take in the tranquil valleys of the French Broad and Davidson rivers. A magnificent view includes the distant Mount Pisgah.

A short trail begins at the inn and climbs to the top of the falls, where a small wooden bridge spans the spring-fed creek. With water rushing just inches below, you overlook a stream winding its way to the French Broad River, which borders the property. Surrounded by the melody of rippling water, you can watch the sun set behind the Pisgah Ridge Mountains.

Key Falls is a low-volume falls, but its modest supply of water is amplified by some 40 stair-step ledges. This results in the hundreds of small cascades that form the 80-foot waterfall. The creek runs under the road and feeds the picturesque pond beside the Key Falls Inn. The pond has two docks for fishing or just sitting and taking in this enchanting scene.

Key Falls is part of 35 acres surrounding the Key Falls Inn, run by Clark and Patricia Grosvenor. The quaint bed-and-breakfast establishment was once the home of Charles Patton, one of the committeemen who laid out the town of Brevard in 1861. Constructed of wood, sand, and rock from the nearby mountainside, the home was started in 1860 but was not finished until after the Civil War in 1868. While the site was not involved in any battles, the open field beside the inn is believed to have served as an encampment for confederate soldiers.

The large Victorian farmhouse was opened as a bed-and-breakfast in 1989. It is the perfect place to rest tired muscles after a full day of waterfall hiking. Nestled in a peaceful valley, it is hard to imagine a more ideal setting for a country inn. The gracious owners offer genuine hospitality, making guests feel like part of the family. If you leave hungry after one of Patricia Grosvenor's delicious breakfasts, you have only yourself to blame.

DIRECTIONS: **From the chamber of commerce building (35 West Main Street) in downtown Brevard, go left on North Broad (East US 64) for 0.9 mile. Make a right on Old H-Ville Highway (Old US 64) and follow it for 2.7 miles. Go right on Everett Road for 0.4 mile and then right again on Seven Springs Road just past the entrance to the Key Falls Inn. The falls are on the left, 0.2 mile up the hill. Park at the base of the falls. The trailhead is 100 yards back down the road on the right.**

**(Although Key Falls is on private land, the owners at the Key Falls Inn are glad to share this beautiful waterfall with the public. Their number is 828-884-7559)**

# CONNESTEE FALLS

$\left[\text{0.4 MILE ROUND-TRIP, MODERATE}\right]$

Connestee Falls is often referred to as a double, or twin, falls. Actually, it is a three-tiered falls that is joined at its base by Batson Creek Falls, a separate waterfall that enhances the appeal of a hike to Connestee Falls. The two cascades are viewed together from a well-maintained trail that leads to the bottom of Connestee Falls.

Emanating from Lake Atagahi, Carson Creek pours a hefty 16,000 gallons a minute over three rock ledges that form Connestee Falls. The modest Carson Creek broadens into a 25-foot wide drape of roaring water as it drops over the first and most precipitous ledge. The waters plunge a total of 110 feet before merging with the output from Batson Creek.

Originating from Lake Ticoa, Batson Creek emerges from the south to glide over a granite dome and also drops 110 feet, creating Batson Creek Falls. Batson Creek Falls has less volume than Connestee Falls. However, when the creeks converge and are squeezed between two rock walls, the result is a wild sluice of water know as Silver Slip. The consolidated waters journey north and eventually join the French Broad River.

Carson Creek was named after Revolutionary War veteran John Carson. He began his military career fighting the Cherokee Indians until a greater enemy came along, the South Carolina Tories. In 1795, after the war for independence was won, Carson moved to Transylvania County and acquired a large parcel of land adjacent to the creek that bears his name.

The land changed hands many times during the ensuing years. William Probart Poor, Brevard's prominent judge, once paid $5 for 100 acres on Carson Creek, which included a then unknown shoals. This shoals later became known as Connestee Falls. Probart Street in Brevard was once named Poor Street in honor of Judge Poor. Due to local objection, the name was changed to the judge's middle name. It seems no one liked the idea of living on Poor Street.

In 1870, a gristmill was constructed at the lip of the falls. A photo hanging in the old Connestee Falls Realty Office showed the mill perched upon the ledge overlooking Connestee Falls. The realty office has since been razed.

Connestee Falls got its name from a beautiful Cherokee Indian princess who jumped to her death after her white husband was lured back to live among his people. It has been rumored that her brokenhearted spirit still roams the scene of her demise. On moonlit nights at the place where the two waterfalls become one, you would not be the first to catch a glimpse of the woeful Princess Connestee.

*Note:* Connestee Falls is currently privately owned and maintained. It is still accessible to the public. You can view the falls from the top but not walk to the base.

DIRECTIONS: **From the chamber of commerce building (35 West Main Street) in downtown Brevard, go half a block and take US 276 south for 6 miles to Connestee Falls. There is a large parking lot on the right serving both the Connestee Falls Realty Office and the trail to the falls.**

# WATERFALLS IN DUPONT STATE FOREST

**HOOKER FALLS:** [0.5 MILE ROUND-TRIP, EASY]

**TRIPLE FALLS AND HIGH FALLS** [1.75 MILES ROUND-TRIP, MODERATE]

**BRIDAL VEIL FALLS:** [4 MILES ROUND-TRIP, MODERATE]

Many people come to DuPont, the most visited of North Carolina's state forests, to see its waterfalls. The 10,300-acre state forest south of Brevard was established in. Outdoor enthusiasts and the grassroots organization Friends of the Falls played a big role in saving the area's waterfalls from development in 2000, when the forest was expanded. The state forest includes the upland plateau of the Little River Valley, which is mostly mixed hardwood forest with sections of white pine. Along with the waterfalls, some of DuPont's highlights include the exposed granite domes, like on the 3,600-foot Stone Mountain, and the picturesque Lake Julia.

The state forest encompasses over 80 miles of trails for horseback riders, hikers, and mountain bikers. In addition to the four waterfalls on the Little River that are listed here, there are also two waterfalls on Grassy Creek, Wintergreen Falls and Grassy Creek Falls. Maps are available from several merchants in town, such as Highland Books, Sycamore Cycles, and Backcountry Outdoors. As of this writing, facilities are limited to picnic areas, parking lots, and portable toilets. Camping is not yet available.

Hooker Falls requires the shortest hike and provides handicapped access. Part of the original land acquisition for the state forest, Hooker Falls is a popular swim-

*Bridal Veil Falls, DuPont State Forest*

ming hole and the former site of a gristmill. Start the hike by ignoring the chain across the gate (it's for cars) and following the wide path marked "Hooker Falls Road." When you intersect the paved handicapped access, bear left staying on the dirt/gravel path. At the top of the falls, continue straight for a good view from an observation area. The 13-foot waterfall drops over a very wide ledge and eventually flows into Cascade Lake. Hooker Falls is considered the fourth waterfall on the Little River.

Triple Falls and High Falls—numbers three and two on the Little River, respectively—are upstream from Hooker Falls. From the same parking lot, walk across the bridge over the Little River and to the other side of the road. Descend left to the river. Follow the trail upstream as it parallels the river and remains level for the first part of the hike. Following a bend to the right, you will ascend steeply. At about 0.3 mile, you can view Triple Falls to the left from the viewing area or to the right from the picnic shelter. A steep and slippery side trail up further on the left marked "To Falls" takes you to the pool between the second and third drop. Triple Falls' three separate tiers add up to 120 feet.

Continue upstream and uphill for another 0.5 mile to reach High Falls. The trail will intersect High Falls Trail, where you need to head left. At the next trail intersection, go right and up a moderately steep climb to view High Falls. The steps to the right lead up to High Falls Shelter for an excellent view. There is also a steep, slippery trail that descends to the pool at the base of the falls. High Falls, the tallest in DuPont State Forest, slides down a granite dome for about 150 feet. The original 7,600 acres of state forest was expanded to include High Falls and Triple Falls in 2000.

Bridal Veil, the first waterfall on the Little River, requires a longer hike than the others (from a different parking area) but is well worth the trip. From the Fawn Lake Access Area, pass the yellow gate next to the information board, reach the sign marking Reasonover Creek Road, and go right walking under the power lines. At the marked intersection, take a left on the wide Conservation Road. You will see a green metal gate and the Shortcut Trail on the left, then walk parallel to an old airport runway and hangar, and finally pass Camp Summit Road, a house, and Lake Julia Road, all on the right. At an unmarked fork, bear left toward an open field and a trail sign about 100 feet away and take a left on Bridal Veil Falls Road (passing a barn on the left). The gravel road ends, but continue straight ahead on the 0.1-mile trail through pine trees toward the falls.

This waterfall, with its unusual overhanging top and long sliding lower section, is on a 2,200-acre tract on the south side of the state forest, which was part of the 2000 acquisition. You can walk under the four-foot overhang, sunbathe on large, rock slabs, and enjoy the pool at the base.

DIRECTIONS: **From the chamber of commerce building (35 West Main Street) in downtown Brevard, go south on US 276 (about 9.8 miles beyond the city limits) to Cedar Mountain. When you reach the post office in Cedar Mountain, continue another 0.9 mile and look for the brown sign directing you to DuPont State Forest, taking a left on Cascade Lake Road. (If you miss the turn, you will enter South Carolina in 1.5 miles.) For Hooker, Triple, and High Falls, you'll pass the parking area for Corn's Mill Shoals after 1 mile; then after another 1.5 miles, turn right onto Staton Road. Travel another 2.2 miles, passing the Agfa plant and reaching the gravel parking area marked "Hooker Falls" on the left, just after the bridge over the Little River. (*Note:* Currently, you must walk across the bridge over the Little River and cross to the other side of Staton Road to reach the trail for Triple Falls and High Falls. However, in December of 2002, funding was appropriated for a foot/horse bridge over the Little River. This will alleviate road crossing.) For Bridal Veil Falls, turn right on Reasonover Road after only 0.1 mile on Cascade Lake Road. Follow this road for 2.8 miles to Fawn Lake Access Area (at the brown sign). Turn left and go uphill, passing four large stone pillars, and then take an immediate left, in less than 0.1 mile, into the gravel parking area.**

# RAVEN CLIFF FALLS

$\left[\text{4.4 MILES ROUND-TRIP, STRENUOUS}\right]$

**M**atthews Creek pours over the top of Raven Cliff and plunges 420 feet to the valley that lies between Coldbranch Mountain and Caesar's Head Mountain. South Carolina's tallest and most breathtaking waterfall, Raven Cliff Falls, is just over the border with North Carolina—so we elected to include it. Raven Cliff is a combination of sheer drops, rushing torrents, lazy pools, sliding fans, and racing cascades. Matthews Creek then joins the Middle Saluda as it carves its way through the valley called the Dismal, named for its stifling heat.

The creek begins with a 30-foot freefall into a pool, and then rushes around both sides of a huge boulder to form two long cascades. This is followed by an 80-foot drop onto a massive granite shelf, a 40-foot sliding fan, and several more cascades and smaller falls.

For those who enjoy a hearty hike, getting to Raven Cliff Falls is half the fun. The trail (#11, red blazes) alternates between modest inclines, level ground, and steep descents as you hike through the undulating topography. After approximately 0.75 mile, you reach a ridge typically buffeted by a strong wind. At an altitude of over 3,200 feet, you have a 100-mile view of the Piedmont below. From here you can see Paris Mountain, Blue Rock, and Table Rock beyond the Greenville Watershed.

The path then drops through a rhododendron thicket, with a rushing creek in earshot. After several descending switchbacks, the trail ends at an observation deck. The falls are viewed across a wide, open valley. Although you are approximately 0.5 mile from the falls, binoculars are not necessary to enjoy the panoramic scene. *(Note:* There is also a trail to a suspension bridge at the top of the falls, which requires additional hiking miles.)

Raven Cliff Falls and the surrounding acreage was owned and preserved by the Moore and Mills families of South Carolina. It was donated to the state in 1981 and is now part of the Caesar's Head State Park. The predominant feature of the park and one of South Carolina's most famous landmarks is Caesar's Head, a massive granite formation which some think resembles the head of Julius Caesar. Although this sounds like a reasonable explanation for the derivation of the name, there are those that believe the famous cliff obtained its name from the Indian word for chieftain, which is sachem. Whatever the origin, Caesar's Head State Park offers hiking, backpacking, a well-maintained trail system, and a magnificent view from Caesar's Head Lookout.

*Raven Cliff Falls*

Stop in at the visitor center before beginning your hike. The trail is constantly being maintained, although major changes are not in the plans. If funding comes through, the park may re-route sections of the trail to provide more vantage points to the falls.

DIRECTIONS: **From the chamber of commerce building (35 West Main Street) in downtown Brevard, take US 276 for 14.1 miles (8 miles past Connestee Falls) south to Raven Cliff Falls in South Carolina. The parking area on the left is reached shortly (2 miles) after crossing the state line, but it is easy to miss because the only sign is not readily visible for motorists traveling south from Brevard. Cars parked along the roadway will indicate the correct location. If you reach the park office, you've gone about 1 mile too far. The well-marked trailhead is on the right side of the road opposite the parking area.**

# fourteen PISGAH FOREST

**T**RANSYLVANIA MEANS "across the woods" in Latin. Most of Transylvania County's 250,000 acres are forested, so the translation is a fitting one. The county's small community of Pisgah Forest exists because of these woodlands. The town is centered around the Carr Lumber Company, which, in the early part of the nineteenth century, purchased a 30-year contract for timber rights to forest property on George Vanderbilt's Biltmore Estate. This land became the nucleus of the Pisgah National Forest. Today, trains still travel to and from the community of Pisgah Forest, carrying freight for the Carr Lumber Company.

About 83,000 acres of Transylvania County is held by Pisgah National Forest. Established in 1916, it is the oldest national forest in the eastern U.S. The vast woodlands of Pisgah and Nantahala National Forests cover more than one million acres spread over twelve North Carolina counties, making it the state's largest public natural resource.

Pisgah was the Biblical mountain from which Moses first looked upon the Promised Land (Deuteronomy 34:1). Similarly, this verdant wonderland held great promise for George Vanderbilt, the visionary who saw its potential.

In the late 1800s, Vanderbilt began acquiring land in the area around Asheville for his fabulous Biltmore Estate, fashioned to recall a sixteenth-century French chateau. He purchased farms and estates, eventually buying more than 125,000 acres. These vast holdings consisted of lush mountain timberland, including Mount Pisgah, a 5,721-foot peak.

Vanderbilt initially hired conservationist Gifford Pinchot to manage his forests and game preserve. Pinchot (who later became governor of Pennsylvania and the first Chief of the Forest Service) planned and oversaw the renovation of Vanderbilt's forest, much of which was badly eroded. His was the first comprehensive forest management system in the Western Hemisphere.

Pinchot's success with the Biltmore timberland encouraged Vanderbilt to purchase additional acreage around Mount Pisgah. Many of the primary ideas of American forestry began and developed in the forests of the Biltmore Estate. Pinchot was influential in the establishment of the Forest Service in 1905.

Pinchot's successor at Biltmore was the famous German forester, Carl A. Schenck. Known as the Father of American Forestry, Dr. Schenck established this

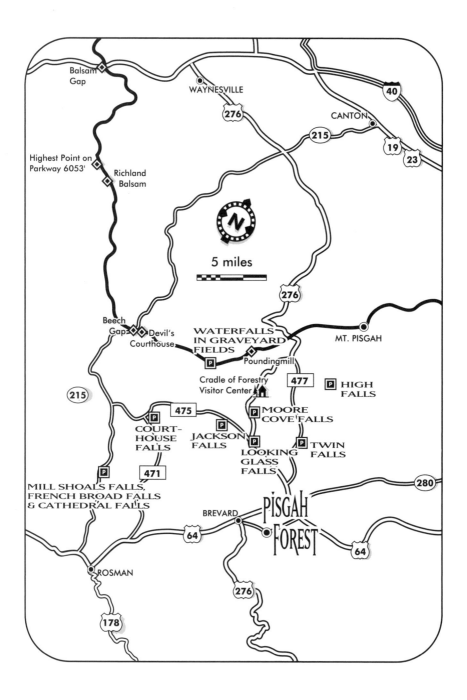

country's first school of forestry in 1898 at the Biltmore Estate. Under Vanderbilt's sponsorship, Schenck started the school to answer the questions of his inquisitive apprentices. The school met at the Biltmore Estate in the winter months; summer sessions were held in Pisgah Forest. With the onset of World War I, Biltmore Forest School graduated its last class, having supplied the United States with many of its early foresters.

After George Vanderbilt's death in 1914, much of his forestland was deeded to, or purchased by, the government. Thus, Biltmore Estate property became one of the first tracts of the Pisgah National Forest. Some of the original Biltmore Estate land was also allocated to the Blue Ridge Parkway.

Pisgah National Forest is comprised of the Pisgah, Toecane, French Broad, and Grandfather Ranger Districts. The Pisgah Ranger District (156,103 acres) is the flagship of all of North Carolina's national forest districts, and one of the most visited. In this district alone, there are over 400 miles of trails and several outstanding attractions and historic firsts.

In 1968, Congress passed the Cradle of Forestry in America Act, which set aside 64,000 acres within the Pisgah National Forest to commemorate the birthplace of Carl Schenck's Biltmore Forest School. The act designated the school as a National Natural Historic Site. Named the Cradle of Forestry in America, the school has been restored and reconstructed to offer visitors a fine exhibit of the history of the first scientific forestry practiced in America.

The exhibit consists of two interpretive trails off US 276. The Biltmore Forest Campus Trail is a 0.9-mile loop that takes the visitor past original as well as reconstructed buildings of the forest school. The campus consisted of mountain cabins and farm homes that were part of an area know historically as the Pink Beds community. The Black Forest lodges, which were used to house the rangers, were replicas of those built in Germany's Black Forest.

There was also a blacksmith shop, a commissary, and the one-room community schoolhouse. The schoolhouse was also the church, where Schenck was known to preach from time to time. He even donated an organ, hoping, he said, to "improve the singing." Alumni of the Biltmore Forest School funded the reconstruction of the school in 1966.

In 1908, the Biltmore Forest Fair was organized to demonstrate the work being done at the school. The 1-mile Forest Festival Trail features exhibits similar to those seen at the fair, including a 1900 steam-powered sawmill and a 1915 climax logging locomotive.

Near the Cradle of Forestry, Pink Beds adorns a mountain valley at 3,250 feet below Pisgah Ledge. The pink is in reference to the pink phlox, laurel, rhododendron, and wild azaleas (known locally as mountain honeysuckle) that cover the highland area in late spring and early summer. The scenic spot has wonderful picnic facilities.

One of the most visited spots in the Pisgah Ranger District is Sliding Rock Falls, where Dr. Schenck's forestry students once enjoyed a breakneck ride down what has been called "the fastest 60 feet in the mountains." At Sliding Rock, the waters of Looking Glass Creek flow at 11,000 gallons per minute over an eel-slick rock formation, plummeting the intrepid adventurer into an icy, seven-foot-deep pool. The spot was once known as Slick Rock by locals, who enjoyed having it to themselves. Now they must share this popular attraction with the thousands of tourists who come here every year. This is a great people-watching spot; even if you're not bold enough to take the plunge yourself, you'll enjoy watching those who do.

Another rock whose presence dominates the Pisgah Ranger District is Looking Glass Rock. This 1,700-foot granite monolith watches over the woods like a giant sentinel. The Cherokee called it the devil's looking glass because of the way the winter sunlight reflected off the frozen side of the mountain.

The Pisgah Ranger District lies within the annual migratory path of the Monarch butterflies, their path crossing the Blue Ridge Parkway between the Looking Glass Rock Parking Area (milepost 417) and Wagon Road Gap (milepost 411). These stunning orange and black insects are the only butterflies that migrate on a regular basis. In September, they fly south to Mexico, where they breed in the spring. Their offspring return to the starting point, usually somewhere in New York, Pennsylvania, or Ontario.

One of the largest fish hatcheries in the East is located on the Davidson River in the Pisgah Ranger District. Operated by the North Carolina Wildlife Resources Commission, the hatchery raises thousands of trout each year. They are used to stock the streams of the forest from March through August. The hatchery raises brook (speckled), brown, and rainbow trout, as well as an unusual golden trout that was developed here.

The Bent Creek Experimental Forest on the north edge of the Pisgah Ranger District is home to a number of state champion trees. Part of the original Biltmore Estate acreage, it was designated by the Forest Service for research on the regeneration of Southern hardwoods.

Brochures, maps, and information on all of the Pisgah Ranger District attractions can be obtained at the ranger station just inside the district on US 276. The rangers are friendly and helpful. Winter hours are from 8 a.m. until 4:30 p.m., Monday through Friday. The station is open on weekends from April through October.

Gifford Pinchot's philosophy was that national forests exist because the people want them. Because of men such as Pinchot, Carl Schenck, and George Vanderbilt, these forests have been preserved. The waterfalls of the Pisgah Ranger District of the Pisgah National Forest are among its most enticing and beautiful features. Some of the falls are easily accessible, while others require a bit more time and effort to reach. Whatever level of adventure you seek, you're sure to enjoy the waterfalls in this beautiful national forest.

# MILL SHOALS FALLS, FRENCH BROAD FALLS, AND CATHEDRAL FALLS

[0.6 MILE ROUND-TRIP, EASY]

Within the Balsam Grove Area of Pisgah National Forest, two watersheds converge behind Living Waters (an operation of There is More Ministries) to form a double waterfall. The North Fork of the French Broad River flows from the northwest and tumbles over a river-wide rock shelf, creating a 60-foot curtain of water called French Broad Falls. Shoal Creek joins the French Broad from the northeast a short distance downstream as Mill Shoals Falls, the site of an old mill house built by William (Bill) McCall around 1900.

These waterfalls are among the easiest and most accessible in the area. Plus, you drive right past them on the way to Courthouse Falls. Just leave the parking area, and walk left, past the chalet building and along the shoulder of NC 215 for about 40 yards. Turn right down an old roadbed to the river. This puts you behind the ministry buildings. (*Note:* The steps behind the chalet building have been blocked off for safety reasons.) You can stand on one of the many rocks at the base of the falls to view the 180-degree panorama of falling water. The roar from the waterfalls drowns out all sounds from the nearby road, giving the visitor the impression of being in the middle of the wilderness.

Further downstream, you will find the 20-foot Cathedral Falls, also called Bird Rock Falls by locals and tourist literature. The name came from the 100-foot granite cliff that served the nesting needs for hundreds of barn swallows.

*Mill Shoals Falls*

DIRECTIONS: **From the Pisgah Ranger Station in Pisgah Forest, travel south on US 276 for 1.4 miles to US 64. Head west on US 64 for 12 miles past Brevard, to Rosman. Turn right onto NC 215 and drive north for about 8 miles. Living Waters Ministries will be on the left; park in their lot. The waterfalls are on private land, so ask permission if possible before viewing. (*Note:* The parking lot will be full if there is a retreat going on.)**

# COURTHOUSE FALLS

[0.6 MILE ROUND-TRIP, EASY]

Courthouse Falls is also called Coon Dog Falls. While on the hunt, a hound was swept away by the current and inadvertently took the plunge. Unbelievably, this cataract was successfully descended by daredevil kayakers who, like the lucky hound, lived to bark about it.

Flowing through the Balsam Grove Area of Pisgah National Forest, Courthouse Creek is a major tributary of the North Fork of the French Broad River. Courthouse Creek charges through Summey Cove picking up speed as the gradient increases.

The forceful water drops over a series of 5-foot ledges before reaching the precipice, where it is squeezed between rock outcroppings and its power is released down a vertical rock face. The result is the magnificent, 50-foot Courthouse Falls. The last 10 feet free falls into a cauldron of bubbling, dark-green water. The granite walls at the base of the waterfall have been eroded by the circular flow of the current, creating an interesting whirlpool effect.

The Summey Cove Trail leads to Courthouse Creek Falls. It follows the creek along an abandoned railroad bed left over from World War I logging days. While you could go on walking along this level trail for several miles, you want to take a left at the trail marker for the falls. This will lead you down a switchback and then a wooden staircase to the base of the falls.

Courthouse Creek originates around Devil's Courthouse Mountain. Cherokee Indian legend tells of a giant slant-eyed devil named Judaculla who resided deep inside the mountain. Within his dark legal chambers, Judaculla passed final

*Courthouse Falls*

judgment on departing souls. This gateway to the spirit world was held in reverence by the Cherokee people, and the waters that emerged were considered sacred.

DIRECTIONS: **From the Pisgah Ranger Station in Pisgah Forest, travel south on US 276 for 1.4 miles to US 64. Head west on US 64 for 12 miles past Brevard, to Rosman. Turn right onto NC 215 and drive north for 10 miles. Turn right on FS 140 (Courthouse Creek Road). Follow this gravel road for 3 miles. Immediately after the fourth bridge, park in the small pulloff on the right. The Summey Cove trailhead is across the road to the right of Courthouse Creek.**

# TWIN FALLS

$\left[ \text{3.8 MILES ROUND-TRIP, EASY} \right]$

Everyone likes buy-one-get-one-free specials at the grocery store because you get double the goods for the same price. This is also true for Twin Falls. On this hike, you get two distinct waterfalls for your efforts; and like fraternal twins, each waterfall has its own special characteristics.

The first waterfall, fed by springs from Rich Mountain, is an 80-foot cascade. The trail crosses at the base of the waterfall, giving you an excellent view as the moderate volume leaps over the edge high above. The water splashes its way down ledges, but there are rocks in the creek at the base that allow you to stay dry if you are photographing the scene.

The second waterfall is just 30 yards from the first. The low volume drift from this fall is light and airy, trailing down 75 feet like a bride's veil. The water collects at the base to form a small rivulet, which joins its twin's creek a short distance down the cove. The creek flows adjacent to the Buckhorn Gap Trail, eventually merging with Avery Creek.

Although these falls are becoming increasingly popular, you will most likely be alone on this walk because they do not appear on the trail maps available at the ranger station. Follow the blue blazes, then the yellow blazes of Avery Creek Trail for 0.9 mile. This is also a horsetrail so be sure to follow the footpath signs. Take the orange-blazed Buckhorn Gap Trail for 0.6 mile to the Twin Falls Loop Trail, which is blue blazed and circles around in either direction for 0.4 mile to both falls.

We keep our young children interested on long hikes by playing a game we call Keeper of the Bridge. When we come to a bridge, the Keeper blocks the path and won't allow passage until each person solves a riddle. If you play the game on this trail, have some riddles handy because there are nine stream crossings, seven with log bridges. (If you're not adept at solving riddles, this could be a three-day hike!)

DIRECTIONS: **From the Pisgah Ranger Station in Pisgah Forest, travel 0.6 mile north on US 276, turn right on FS 477, and follow this gravel road for 2.5 miles. (At 1.7 miles, you will pass the horse stables; continue up the hill for 0.8 mile.) Park on the right at the trailhead.**

# LOOKING GLASS FALLS

[ NO HIKE NECESSARY ]

Is there such a thing as *the* classic waterfall? Most people agree that Looking Glass Falls is the epitome of a postcard waterfall. Because of its easy access, Looking Glass Falls is a major tourist attraction, one of the most well-known falls in the eastern United States.

This waterfall is a symbol for the Pisgah National Forest. The cover of the "Pisgah Area Trail Map" sports a photo of Looking Glass Falls. The image shows up on many things you buy. And, you can get a postcard showing the classic waterfall.

Holding rainwater like a sponge, the forest cover atop Looking Glass Rock gives rise to the creeks that feed the falls. The high volume from Looking Glass Creek creates a 30-feet-wide undivided rush of water that surges over a 65-foot sheer drop. As the waters dive into the pool at the base, a misty spray drifts upward to coat the sides of the towering granite shelf.

Looking Glass Creek eventually flows into the Davidson River. The Davidson River south of Avery Creek is stocked from the nearby fish hatchery. In the early spring, you will find the streams busy with anglers trying their luck for brook, brown, and rainbow trout. The hatchery raises and stocks 60,000 trout in the streams of the Pisgah National Forest each year.

Many present-day highways in the Pisgah National Forest follow the old railroad beds of the bygone era. US 276, the road past the falls, follows almost the exact location of an old railroad bed that transported timber out of the forest to the mills. In the early 1920s, the Carr Lumber Company built and maintained 75 miles of railroad in what is now the Pisgah National Forest.

For 30 years, lumber was one of the most thriving industries in Transylvania County. It was not uncommon to see three to four million board feet of lumber stacked around the Pisgah Forest Mill. The double-band mill was capable of sawing up to 100,000 board feet a day.

DIRECTIONS: **From the Pisgah Ranger Station in Pisgah Forest, travel 4 miles north on US 276. The parking area is on the right. You can observe the falls from your car or walk the steps to the base of the falls.**

# MOORE COVE FALLS

[1.3 MILES ROUND-TRIP, EASY]

**M**oore Cove Falls could be an all day-trip—not because it's a long hike, but because it's such a serene and restful place that you could easily lose track of time. The gentle waters of Moore Creek dribble over a small series of stair-step ledges and then rain down 50 feet over a sheer drop to the creek below. The trail goes behind the docile curtain into a large granite cove. You can sit and look through the falling water without getting wet. It's like watching a summer rain through a window. The cool nook provides plenty of seating and could easily accommodate a group of friends.

The trail to the falls is a natural obstacle course—lots of diversity and lots of fun. The beginning of the trail meanders between house-sized granite boulders that are laced with veins of quartz. Further along the trail there is a wooden slat bridge, some soggy ground, and several creek crossings, which require you to rock hop and negotiate log bridges. Near the falls, you have to duck under a strange-looking tree, growing horizontally for 20 feet out of the side of a hill before turning upward for another 50 feet.

The falls were named for Adam Q. Moore, a onetime U.S. commissioner and justice of the peace. Moore owned 50 acres along Looking Glass Creek. Although he only owned the land for three years, his name was commonly used and became permanently attached to the creek and the falls. He sold his entire parcel in 1880 to the King family, who conveyed ownership to the Vanderbilt estate in 1901 for the modest sum of $155.

The trail follows Moore Creek to the falls. There is a small, primitive camping site just downstream within view of the falls. For those who like to fall asleep to the pitter-patter of rain, Moore Cove Falls could be your ticket to dreamland.

DIRECTIONS: From the Pisgah Ranger Station in Pisgah Forest, go 5 miles north on US 276. Moore Cove Falls is 1 mile up the road from Looking Glass Falls. Park in the area beside the concrete bridge on the right side of the road. Walk over the bridge to find the trailhead between the two wooden posts.

# HIGH FALLS

[ 4 MILES ROUND-TRIP, STRENUOUS ]

High Falls is not . . . high! It is also not particularly wide, or powerful, or distinctive, or easy to access. But of all the things High Falls is not, the most important virtue is that it's not frequently visited.

The trail can be confusing and you have to wade across South Mills River. Many people simply can't find the falls. This tranquil seclusion makes High Falls the ideal oasis for the urban hermit wishing to get away from it all.

About 1 mile from the trailhead, go left on the small side trail just before the old concrete bridge. Continue 0.6 mile until you get to South Mills River. Ford the 20-foot-wide river, which can be one to three feet deep. Continuing 0.4 mile on the trail, you will pass a high waterfall dropping into the creek from the left, but this is not High Falls. Keep walking down the soggy trail a short distance to the actual High Falls.

You'll soon see the river gushing over a large jumble of rocks creating 30 feet of churning chaos. In sharp contrast to the agitated whitewater, there is a calm pool at the base—as big as a swimming pool.

Many gristmills and sawmills once graced the streams and rivers of these mountains, so it would be easy to conclude this was the derivation for the name South Mills River. Actually, the Revolutionary War veteran Major William Mills named the river after himself. In 1787, he was awarded 640 acres in return for his military service.

The headwaters of South Mills River meander through the famous Pink Beds in the Pisgah National Forest. At an altitude of over 3,200 feet, the Pink Beds are an unusual highland bog. The 36-square-mile tract of land could have gotten its name from the startling array of rosebay rhododendrons, mountain laurel, wild azaleas, and great masses of wild pink phlox—a botanist's paradise. Or, another source of the name could have been the pink rock that was once mined in the area.

DIRECTIONS: From the Pisgah Ranger Station in Pisgah Forest, travel 10 miles north on US 276. Go right on FS 1206 (Yellow Gap Road) and follow the gravel road for 3.3 miles. Go right again on FS 476 (South Mills River Road) and travel 1.3 miles to the end of the road. The trailhead leaves from the lower end of the parking area.

# WATERFALLS IN GRAVEYARD FIELDS

UPPER YELLOWSTONE
FALLS: $\left[\text{3.2 MILES ROUND-TRIP, EASY}\right]$

SECOND FALLS: $\left[\text{0.8 MILE ROUND-TRIP, MODERATE}\right]$

**G**et Along Little Doggie," "Happy Trails to You," "The Wayward Wind". . . it's easy to find yourself humming Western songs on your way through Graveyard Fields. With a little imagination, you can convince yourself that you are in the West rather than a national forest in North Carolina. In contrast to the surrounding abundant timberland, the barren, rock-strewn landscape is only sparsely dotted with scraggly trees.

At an elevation of 5,120 feet, Graveyard Fields was named for its unique terrain. Fallen trees and stumps, which once blanketed the area, were covered with moss and spruce needles, resembled gravestones. A fire in 1925 destroyed 25,000 acres, leaving a desolate open pocket of land, which has recovered slowly.

Follow the paved trail for 0.2 mile through a dense rhododendron thicket to the wooden bridge spanning the Yellowstone Prong of the Pigeon River's East Fork. The trail left leads to Upper Yellowstone Falls. The trail right leads to Second Falls.

The trail to Upper Yellowstone Falls follows Yellowstone Prong. While mostly flat, the path occasionally joins washed-out storm beds and is rocky in places. At the trail's end, when you see a small current of rushing water, you may think "Is that it?" Cross over the channel and walk around the bend to view Upper Yellowstone Falls.

Yellowstone Prong emerges between two rock masses and pours 50 feet down a narrow stone channel. The towering rock wall, which directs the current, is not typical gray granite, but pale pink in color. The surrounding walls create a small canyon, adding to the Western-type landscape.

Second Falls, also called Little Yellowstone Falls, is only 0.2 mile from the bridge over the Yellowstone Prong. The trail makes a sharp right and descends

*Second Falls, Graveyard Fields*

steeply through an area washed out by drainage to the base of the falls. Second Falls is also visible from the Parkway before you reach Graveyard Fields Overlook.

The current is wider than Upper Yellowstone Falls and it drops over a series of three ledges for a total of 60 feet. As the water proceeds off the last ledge, it fans to a width of 25 feet. Unlike Upper Yellowstone Falls, the waters combine at the bottom to form an inviting swimming hole.

There is a third waterfall on Yellowstone Prong called Yellowstone Falls. It appears on some maps and in some reference material, but there is no maintained trail and the access is dangerously steep. Forest rangers do not recommend visiting it.

DIRECTIONS: **From the Pisgah Ranger Station in Pisgah Forest, travel 13.4 miles north on US 276 to the Blue Ridge Parkway. Go south on the Parkway for 7.1 miles to Graveyard Fields Overlook (milepost 419). The trail leaves from the parking area down a wooden stairway.**

# JACKSON FALLS

$$\left[\text{0.6 MILE ROUND-TRIP, EASY}\right]$$

Jackson Falls does not appear on any of the official trail maps because it was only discovered some 30 years ago. No one knew the falls existed until the early 1970s when Ray Jackson cut the logging road to access the timber management area south of Laurel Ridge. His co-workers started calling this waterfall Jackson Falls, and the name stuck. Often waterfalls bear the name of the individual who owns the land or happens to discover the falls. In the case of this waterfall, the honor goes to the timber management administrator. The waterfall is also called Daniel Ridge Falls.

Jackson Falls begins its near-vertical descent down the mountainside 100 feet above the logging road. It cascades, slides, leaps, and free falls over a series of large stone slabs. The moderate volume of water begins as an 8-foot-wide branch and reaches a width of 40 feet by the time it drops to the base. The waters run under the road and continue down the mountain, running into one of the prongs of the Davidson River.

A gravel logging road ascends a hill and leads to the base of Jackson Falls. To the left of the falls, there is a trail marker for Daniel Ridge Trail, a new name for an old trail. Thinking we could get a different view of the falls, we hiked the moderate 0.4-mile slope. From the top, there was no view of the falls due to dense foliage, but the sound effects were great and there was an excellent view of Looking Glass Rock. With water streaming down its sides and reflecting the sunlight, Looking Glass Rock stands like a lonely sentinel, rising 1,700 feet above the forest floor. The Daniel Ridge Trail continues past the top of the falls into the timber management area.

DIRECTIONS: **From the Pisgah Ranger Station in Pisgah Forest, travel 3.5 miles north on US 276 and turn left onto FS 475 (Fish Hatchery Road). After 1.4 miles, you will pass the fish hatchery; the paved road changes to gravel. Take FS 475A, the lower gravel road that follows the river, for 1.9 miles. Continue past Cove Creek Campground for 0.7 mile to the unmarked parking circle on the right. Walk up the road past the gate for 0.3 mile. The falls will be on the left. (This is an active logging area so be sure not to block the locked Forest Service gate.)**

# fifteen LAKE TOXAWAY

IN THE WESTERN PART of Transylvania County, US 64 passes by Lake Toxaway. Toxaway, taken from the Cherokee Indian word Tox-awah, which means "red bird," lies within the valley of Mount Toxaway in the southern Blue Ridge. The original town of Toxaway was actually incorporated in 1901 at the site of present-day Rosman. However, when Lake Toxaway was built and the area around the lake began to be developed, people began to get the two places confused. To make things easier, Joseph Silversteen changed the name of Toxaway to Rosman, in honor of two of his business associates, Mr. Rosenthal and Mr. Omansky.

The modern-day Lake Toxaway is a picture of tranquility. The glimmering surface of the water reflects the lush green of the surrounding forests and mirrors the sapphire blue of the sky. Nestled serenely among the mountains, gracious homes dot the perimeter of the lake.

Imagine: Ladies and gentlemen in elegant attire stroll the beautiful shores of Lake Toxaway, while children roll playfully across the manicured lawns of the opulent Toxaway Inn. Couples in canoes skim lazily across the calm lake. Listen, and you can almost hear their refined voices carrying across the crisp mountain air, or the tinkle of crystal drifting through the open doors of the inn's tasteful dining room like musical notes.

Once, in this remote mountain valley was the Switzerland of America. The rich and famous came in droves, the guest list included such moguls as Edison, Ford, Vanderbilt, Firestone, Reynolds, and Rockefeller. This genteel civilization rode in on the rail, was swept away with a mighty roar, and was reborn on the shimmering waters of present-day Lake Toxaway. The story of how it happened is fascinating.

George Vanderbilt began it all when he built his Biltmore Estate near Asheville in the late 1800s. Suddenly, the remote mountain wilderness of western North Carolina was prime property. Soon, other northern entrepreneurs began to recognize the potential of the area and came to be part of the boom. Among them were J. Frances Hayes and Joseph Silversteen.

Hayes conceived the idea of a resort for millionaires and set about building Lake Toxaway and the Toxaway Inn. He had the genius of foresight to purchase the Transylvania Railroad Company (formerly the Hendersonville & Brevard), for no resort could succeed without a comfortable means of transporting

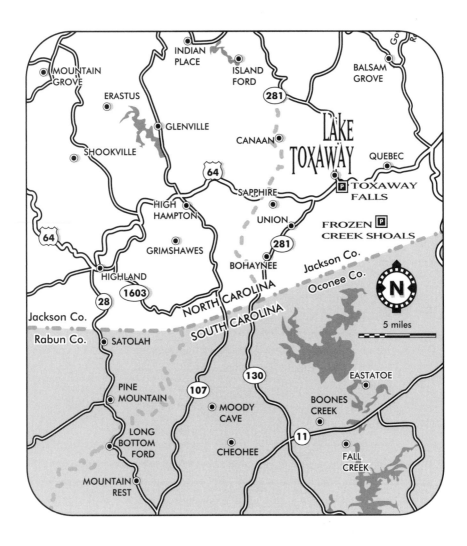

its guests. Transportation in those early days consisted of horse- and ox-drawn wagons along a few questionable roads. Needless to say, the railroad was crucial to the success of Mr. Hayes's venture. In order to ensure the passage of a bond issue to extend the railroad from Brevard to Lake Toxaway, Hayes agreed to build the Franklin Hotel in Brevard.

The rail line that began in Asheville and extended to Toxaway was not an easy feat. It was the steepest railroad system in the United States, but it was essential in transporting affluent tourists to the Toxaway Inn and other area resorts such as the Fairfield Inn, the Sapphire Inn, the Lodge, and the Franklin Hotel. Like the railroad, these magnificent resorts were outstanding accomplishments for their time.

Lake Toxaway was the first artificial lake ever built in the Appalachian Mountains. There was no other lake like it in the eastern United States. Its waters flowed from pure mountain springs and waterfalls of the surrounding unspoiled wilderness. Perched at 3,012 feet, this 640-acre lake, with 14 miles of shoreline, was the largest man-made lake in the world at that time. The earthen dam that held the lake was 500 feet long, 60 feet high, 20 feet wide at the top, and 50 feet thick at the base.

Toxaway Inn, opening in 1903, was an elegant resort, one of the finest of its era. It was built using more than 40 types of wood, all cut from the property. It offered the rare modern conveniences of central heat, indoor plumbing, and elevators. French chefs prepared exquisite cuisine, served on imported china and crystal. Only the finest linens and silver were used. Guests danced the night away in the ballroom and found recreation in the billiard parlor and bowling alley. Those wishing sport could swim, boat, fish, hike, play tennis, or ride horseback.

A Southern Railroad brochure promoted Lake Toxaway as "...a lovely spot, high up in the glorious mountains of western North Carolina, and it will do you good to go there." Many wealthy people agreed. But when the Toxaway Inn was at the height of its splendor, the unpredictable hand of nature swept it all away with the flick of a wrist.

The rains came in the summer of 1916. Western North Carolina was severely flooded and the dam, having no low drainage pipe, was filled to capacity. In early August, a hurricane came ashore from the Gulf of Mexico and moved inland up the Mississippi Valley. The combination of rains from the hurricane and a smaller storm produced another deluge of unprecedented proportions. The surrounding environment was damaged and you can still see debris piles.

The Greenville News of August 14, 1916, reported that, at 7:10 on the evening of August 13, the dam caved and sent a "solid wall of water 30 feet high" down the 16-mile gorge into South Carolina. It was said that the thunderous roar could be heard for miles.

Miraculously, accounts say the only loss of life was a blind mule. The destruction of property, however, was astronomical. Many of the area mills were obliterated as well. The damage suits and litigation lasted for years, mainly because there were those who believed that the dam had been leaking prior to August 13th. It was also shown that the dam was built on top of a spring that had weakened the earthen structure.

Photographs taken around Toxaway Falls prior to the dam break show lush foliage and vegetation across the entire area. The force of an estimated five billion gallons of rushing water uprooted everything growing in its path, including trees four feet in diameter. Boulders the size of trucks were pitched down the gorge like marbles. The present-day site of Toxaway Falls is a 300-foot-wide bare expanse of rock that drops 350 feet to the river below.

Although the Toxaway Inn was not destroyed, the disastrous loss of the lake spelled its demise. Adding to the catastrophe of the dam break, World War I and the Great Depression contributed to the end of the tourist trade. Lake Toxaway was once again a quiet, secluded spot, hidden among the mountains. It would remain so for almost half a century.

The area was revived with the rebuilding of the dam and the lake in 1961. A group of investors, headed by R.D. Heinitsh, Sr., bought the 9,000-acre tract that had surrounded the original resort of Toxaway. The new dam, completed in March of 1961, was 60 feet deep and 300 feet wide at the base with a 60-feet-wide solid granite spillway. The Lake Toxaway Company also began the construction of roads around the lake.

While the Toxaway Inn no longer stands, the Greystone Inn graces the shores of Lake Toxaway as a reminder of the grandeur of that bygone era. Savannah native Lucy Armstrong Moltz spent a summer camping near Lake Toxaway before building this mansion–her second home–in 1915. "I've been around the world twice and I've found no place more beautiful or special," she wrote. In 1985, the six-level Swiss mansion opened as an inn, offering award-winning accommodations.

In the interim between the flood and the rebuilding of Lake Toxaway, the area did not go completely unnoticed. The beauty of the scenery here inspired Hollywood to use the site as a film location. The movie *Tap Roots* with Susan Haywood and Van Heflin was filmed on location here in 1948. The famous Robert Mitchum film *Thunder Road* was made here in 1957.

Lake Toxaway resident Jack Hall was seventeen years old at the time *Thunder Road* was filmed. He remembers playing hookey from school for two weeks in order to assist with the production. Jack vividly recalls the day they filmed the famous scene in which the 1957 Ford crashed over the falls to the river below.

Only, according to Jack, the car didn't exactly fall where it was supposed to. Instead, the plunging vehicle landed to the right of the falls, setting the woods on fire. The wreckage lay there for months, giving souvenir seekers a chance to grab a piece of *Thunder Road*. Jack got the hood ornament and a door handle.

Today, Lake Toxaway is the largest private lake in North Carolina. The Lake Toxaway Company and Country Club are carrying on the exclusive tradition of the Toxaway Inn, offering a luxurious standard of living in a secluded mountain setting. Once again, people come from all around to enjoy the splendor of the lake, the mountains, and the forests.

Fortunately, the majestic mountains and lush forest belong to all of us. They are ours to cherish, along with the region's coursing rivers and streams. Within a radius of a few miles from Lake Toxaway, there are dozens of waterfalls.

# TOXAWAY FALLS

[No hike necessary]

**W**ow, look at that!" is a common reaction from unsuspecting motorists who round the corner on US 64 between Sapphire and Brevard and come face to face with Toxaway Falls. Though the volume of water is low compared to some of the other falls in Transylvania County, the view of the falls and the river gorge below is spectacular. After a full day of waterfall trekking, the tired hiker may also appreciate that Toxaway Falls is visible from the car.

From the dam which impounds Lake Toxaway, the Toxaway River runs under the concrete bridge and the falls begin their near-vertical plunge at three thousand feet above sea level. Water slides 125 feet over a massive dome-shaped granite shelf, and halfway down, a curved rock causes the current to spout upward and form a huge rooster tail. The Toxaway River continues its turbulent path over numerous cascades and cataracts on its 1,500-foot descent through the picturesque Toxaway River Gorge, finally relaxing upon reaching the backwaters of Lake Jocassee.

Many people believe that the falls, river, mountain, and lake were named after the famous Cherokee Indian leader, Toxawah. The name Toxaway was also linked to an Indian settlement in the area; however, the spelling on the old maps and deeds was "Toxawah." Prevailing legend puts the grave of Toxawah at the top of Indian Grave Ridge, which is approximately 0.75 mile from the top of Toxaway Falls.

The destruction from the fateful day of the flood of 1916 is still visible. The sweeping torrent cleared the heavy riverside vegetation and exposed the massive granite domes. The landscape may be altered, but the view from the top of the falls is still breathtaking.

*Toxaway Falls*

DIRECTIONS: Toxaway Falls is just downstream from Lake Toxaway Dam. US 64 goes over the top of the falls. Use the restaurant parking lot just west of the falls for a good view, or use an access point just east of the falls and walk out on the boulders for a closer view. Extreme caution is advised.

# FROZEN CREEK SHOALS

$\left[\right.$ 0.4 MILE ROUND-TRIP, MODERATE $\left.\right]$

For the contemporary adventure seeker, Frozen Creek Shoals is an interesting waterfall with an interesting history. For yesterday's residents of the Ridge Haven Area, the Shoals was the power for a tub mill that was a means of making a living and providing for the family. For others, the Shoals provided many a gallon for some of the finest bootleg whiskey known in these parts.

After purchasing 50 acres on Frozen Creek in 1876, Jim Earl Galloway built a tub mill at the foot of the large shoal to grind corn. A wooden flume was constructed to carry water from the top of the falls to the awaiting turbines below. A tub mill, as opposed to a waterwheel mill, accumulates the flow in a large tub, and then drains the water out the bottom through the turbines. As the water turns the turbines, a system of gears and rods turns the grinding stones, which mill the corn into meal for farmers or mash for moonshiners.

In addition to serving as the major ingredient of the proud and potent product, the crystal-clear water was funneled through the still to aid in the fermentation process. The area became famous for the quality of its moonshine and was a major destination for those who preferred to get their corn from a jar.

In 1924, a Rosman businessman named Dewey Winchester bought the 55-acre tract on Frozen Creek, including the old Galloway Mill. A short distance downstream from the mill, he dammed Frozen Creek to form Frozen Lake and constructed Frozen Lake Lodge.

Frozen Creek got its name because it runs along the west side of a mountain called Frozen Knob, which during winter is often glazed with ice. The site was once known as Mill Shoals, but because this name was so common throughout the county, the name was changed to Frozen Creek Shoals.

A short trail, which winds behind a private home, leads to Frozen Creek Shoals. Frozen Creek drains over a 35-foot high slanting granite shelf, forming the falls. Halfway down the ledge, the flow is partially obstructed by a rock ledge, creating a small rooster tail of water that protrudes off the rock face. The spirited waters quickly settle into a pool at the base where you can see the remnants of the gristmill and its stone foundation. From the lake, Frozen Creek flows into Toxaway Creek on its way to the Toxaway River and Lake Jocassee.

DIRECTIONS: **From Lake Toxaway Dam on US 64 (the location of Toxaway Falls), drive east 6.1 miles and go right onto Frozen Creek Road. After 0.7 mile, bear left and continue for another 3.3 miles. When you see a large wooden-framed home on the right, park on the road's shoulder. You'll hear the waters roar from the roadway, and the ill-defined trailhead is midway between the two telephone poles. (This is private property so permission should be sought if possible.)**

CASHIERS APPEARS TO BE just a crossroads, the junction of US 64 and NC 107. Here, you'll find the only traffic light in town. But there is much more to this quiet resort town than the intersection.

Located on the Eastern Continental Divide at 3,500 feet, Cashiers is surrounded by 20,000 acres of national forest–the Nantahala National Forest and the Pisgah National Forest. For every ten acres of forest, there is one acre of lake, including Lake Glenville, which is considered to be the highest major lake in the eastern U.S.

There are several peaks that rise 1,500 feet above the town. The highest, Yellow Mountain, stands at 5,127 feet above sea level. Cashiers also claims the famous Whiteside Mountain, sharing it with Highlands, even though the mountain is a couple of miles closer to Cashiers. For a great photograph, take US 64 west out of town for 4 miles (before the Jackson County line) and pull over on the right. This area, known as Big View, offers an astounding postcard view of Whiteside Mountain.

If you're interested in history, there are two rocks that are worth a visit–Judaculla Rock and Ellicott's Rock. Judaculla Rock, located on Caney Fork Road, is a 40-foot boulder with pictographs. These symbols may have been carved by Indians, but they have yet to be deciphered. Ellicott's Rock, named for Andrew Ellicott who surveyed the line between North Carolina and South Carolina around 1812, marks the junction of Georgia, South Carolina, and North Carolina. This rock can be reached via the Ellicott Rock Trail (7 miles round-trip) at Ammons Branch Campground.

The attractive shops and fine restaurants of Cashiers are similar to Highlands–antiques and Carolina crafts, country food, and gourmet cuisine–except there are not as many and they are not as crowded. If you only have a little time to shop, go to the Olde Home Place, located on NC 107 just south of the town's main intersection. One stop provides all the mountain treasures you can imagine–homemade goodies, custom-made quilts, and North Carolina pottery. There is even a Christmas room open year-round.

Cashiers has an unusual name, and there are an unusually large number of theories about the origin. There is also a long-standing controversy about which theory is right. The valley could have been named after a lumber company cashier's office or after an original settler who lived in the area, but the stories that involve animals seem to be the most popular.

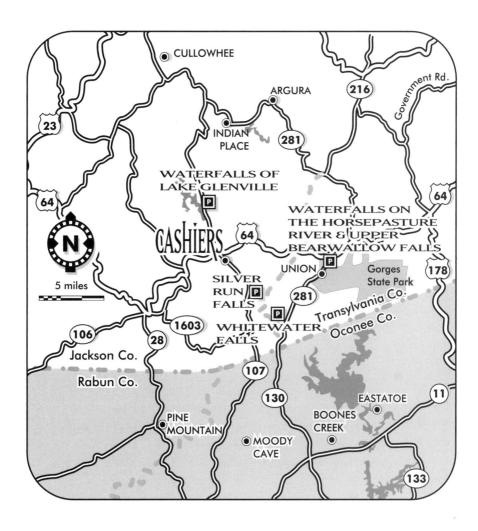

Some people think there was a horse named Cash who wandered off, and a search party yelled "Cash's here" when they found him. Others believe it was a race horse whose prize money earned him the right to spend winters in the valley instead of heading south with the rest of the stock. Change horse to bull, and Cash to Cassius, and you have yet another story about how Cashiers got its name.

The list of theories is long and there doesn't seem to be a consensus. So, here are the facts. Cashiers was settled around 1830 by Colonel John Zachary and James McKinney; but records mention the area as early as 1540 when Hernando de Soto, the Spanish explorer, came through on his way to the Mississippi River.

The Cherokee Indians were here for several generations before the first settlers (Scots and Irish) put up their log cabins in the early 1800s. A hundred years later, many of the South's elite came to Cashiers to escape the heat, and the town's been growing as a resort area ever since. One such summer resident, General Wade Hampton from South Carolina, had a home on Chimney Mountain, which is now the High Hampton Inn and Country Club, one of North Carolina's most exclusive resorts.

Every town has its claim to fame, some have several. Our favorite piece of Cashiers trivia involves the Grimshawes post office, which is the smallest (six by eight) post office in the United States. You can visit the restored building on Whiteside Cove Road.

Cashiers has another claim to fame; it is home to one of the highest waterfalls in the East. It is spectacular, but as you'll discover, the other waterfalls around Cashiers won't be upstaged. Don't miss the waterfall hikes along the Wild and Scenic Horsepasture River, or in North Carolina's newest state park, or on the boat trip around Lake Glenville.

# WHITEWATER FALLS

[0.4 MILE ROUND-TRIP, EASY]

This is the king of waterfalls; it is considered to be the highest cascade east of the Rockies. Whitewater Falls lives up to its title. It is immense and spectacular. The river plunges 411 feet over the sheer granite cliffs of the gorge. It falls, tumbles, and slides. The ground seems to shake as the sound of crashing water echoes in the valley.

Silver Run Creek (where you will find Silver Run Falls) and Little Whitewater Creek join above Whitewater Falls to form the Whitewater River. After the river crosses the border of North Carolina and South Carolina, it drops another 400 feet, creating Lower Whitewater Falls, and then flows into Lake Jocassee.

Whitewater Falls is surrounded by a mix of oak, poplar, maple, and hickory. The highlights of the understory are trilliums and woodland orchids. The constant spray from the falls creates a home for various tropical ferns and mosses.

You can enjoy the falls from an observation point at the end of the paved walkway and then head back to the picnic tables for lunch and a great view of Lake Jocassee. Or, if you have more time, you can explore a portion of the Foothills Trail, which intersects Whitewater Falls Scenic Area at the observation point. The Foothills Trail is an 80-mile path stretching from Table Rock State Park to Oconee State Park.

Descend the 400 steps to the right to reach the Whitewater River. The path to the left from the observation point is also part of the Foothills Trail and fords the river a short distance upstream of Whitewater Falls. (Caution: The brink of the falls is extremely dangerous and many people have lost their lives here.)

**DIRECTIONS: Travel east from Cashiers on US 64 for about 9 miles to NC 281 and turn right. Continue almost to the SC state line, about 9 miles, and turn left at the sign for Whitewater Falls Scenic Area. Follow this 0.2-mile access road to the parking area ($2 fee). The paved trail begins at the north end of the parking lot.**

# WATERFALLS ON THE HORSEPASTURE RIVER

**DRIFT FALLS:** [2.6 MILES ROUND-TRIP, MODERATE]

**TURTLEBACK FALLS:** [2 MILES ROUND-TRIP, MODERATE]

**RAINBOW FALLS:** [2.4 MILES ROUND-TRIP, MODERATE]

**STAIRWAY FALLS:** [4 MILES ROUND-TRIP, STRENUOUS]

Prior to October 27th, 1986, the Horsepasture River was in danger because a power company was planning to build a hydroelectric dam that would terminate the water flow to the falls. But Friends of the Horsepasture River (FROTH), with the help of legislators and state organizations, won their fight to block the project. A section of river 4.5 miles long was designated Wild and Scenic to be protected by the federal government.

The wild river plunges almost 2,000 feet over 6 miles in a dramatic series of wide drops and boulder-filled rapids. Its scenic banks are covered with rhododendrons and hemlocks, and the rare shortia plant can be found here on occasion. Additionally, the Horsepasture River is a waterfall collector's heaven; four outstanding cascades can be seen along this trail.

At the time of publication for this edition, the parking situation was changing along NC 281. You can no longer park alongside the guardrail on the extended shoulder (about 1.8 miles south of US 64). If you are going to overnight on the Horsepasture River, you will be ticketed if you park at the new lot for Gorges State Park. In the spring of 2003, the Forest Service was meeting to plan their own parking lot and access trail. At the parking lot, there should be room for about 10–15 cars, which may not be enough room on summer weekends and holidays; they are currently flagging a trail to tie into the existing one along the river. With this pending, the directions for the parking area and the beginning of the hike are not available. The mileage is estimated using the gated road south of the parking at the state park. There is a Forest Service-built trail parallel to the river once you reach Turtleback Falls; it is well maintained and relatively flat. You can walk upstream to view Drift Falls, which is now posted "no trespassing." The land changed hands in 1998.

It used to be common to see swimmers enjoying Drift Falls in the summer. The locals called it Bohaynee Beach named after the nearby community. There were some adventuresome characters that rode the falls like a commercial super-slide, sailing over rocks on inner tubes. The river glides over an enormous dome into a calm swimming hole; the total drop is 30 feet. Turtleback Falls only drops 20 feet, but the surrounding area is beautiful. The river takes a 90-degree right turn. Upstream of the curve, you'll find the falls, a river-wide, uniform drop over a smooth shelf. Downstream of the curve, just beyond some big boulders, the river disappears.

*Rainbow Falls, Horsepasture River*

In actuality, the Horsepasture's vanishing act is Rainbow Falls, a near-vertical drop of 200 feet. The entire river crashes onto the boulders below, producing a deafening roar. If the sun is just right, you may see colorful arches created in the spray; hence the name, Rainbow Falls.

Few people venture as far as Stairway Falls because there is little or no trail. The user-created path becomes difficult to follow and overgrown in places. After you cross a 10-foot wide creek, hike several hundred yards uphill and locate the side trail (sharp right) that leads down to the river.

The peaceful nature of the falls is captivating, quite a change from the powerful Rainbow Falls. Several stair-steps, averaging 10 feet each, add up to a total drop of just over 50 feet. At one time, it was called Adam Shoals, after a previous owner. His wife is buried to the east of the falls. Her death (in 1879) is puzzling. The coroner stated that she fell into the fireplace of their home, but how she fell is unknown.

DIRECTIONS: **Travel east from Cashiers on US 64 for about 9 miles to NC 281 and turn right. After about 0.8 mile, you'll pass the parking for Gorges State Park. (You can park here if you are going for a day hike.) The new Forest Service parking area is planned to be located about 0.5 mile past the state park's lot. The project will not be complete until 2004. Contact the Highlands Ranger District of Nantahala National Forest for more information about the parking and access trail.**

# UPPER BEARWALLOW FALLS

*[ 3.2 MILES ROUND-TRIP, STRENUOUS ]*

Upper Bearwallow Falls (also called Snakerock Falls), part of North Carolina's newest state park, is accessed by the new Waterfalls Overlook Trail. The 7,100-acre Gorges State Park was dedicated during Labor Day weekend in 1999 and is located between NC 281 and Frozen Creek Road, south of US 64.

The park is characterized by the rugged terrain of the Blue Ridge Escarpment, with dramatic elevation changes up to 2,000 feet in 4 miles, plunging rivers, remote gorges, and sheer rock walls. In the state park, there are over a dozen falls, some on on the Toxaway River and Bearwallow Creek and others on their tributaries and other smaller streams. You can access the spectacular Gorges Section of the Foothills Trail from the other side of the park, where several deep rivers course down into Lake Jocassee.

Upper Bearwallow Falls, just inside park's northwestern boundary, drops about 80 feet in several stair-steps. It is one of the most beautiful waterfalls in the county. The trailhead is at Grassy Ridge on NC 281, just north of the access for waterfalls on the Horsepasture River (which is not part of the state park). Blue circles blaze the trail, which ends at an excellent observation deck complete with benches. This waterfall is one of several on Bearwallow Creek. From the same trailhead, you can follow green circles to six primitive campsites at Ray Fisher Place if you want to spend a night in the area.

The state park is still in the early stage of development, and very few trails are open. Plans include trails to the interior of the park and other waterfalls, as well as a campground and visitor center. It will take time to complete the trail system, and many areas will remain remote. Please do not bushwhack; travel only on marked trails. The state park is home to a large concentration of unique and rare plants. Officials are working hard to protect this incredible natural resource, as well as provide recreation for a variety of users.

DIRECTIONS: **Travel east from Cashiers on US 64 for about 9 miles to NC 281 and turn right. Head south for about 0.7 mile to the state park's lot on the left. There are picnic tables and a portable toilet. Be aware that information and regulations change frequently. Check in at the state park's interim office located at the junction of US 64 and NC 281.**

# WATERFALLS
# OF LAKE GLENVILLE

[ NO HIKE NECESSARY ]

Tired of hiking? Here are three waterfalls—Hurricane Falls, Norton Falls, and Mill Creek Falls—that you can visit by boat. What kind of boat? You name it! Take a canoe or kayak, a ski boat, fishing boat, or pontoon. The folks at the family-owned Signal Ridge Marina (established in 1994) on Lake Glenville will be glad to give you a map, rent you a boat, and help you plan a day of sightseeing. The Glenville Country Store is next door and their deli serves breakfast and lunch.

Each waterfall is located on a different finger of the lake and cascades about 30 or 40 feet, depending on the lake's level. Hurricane Falls is 2 miles south of the marina, and Norton Falls and Mill Creek Falls are 2 and 4 miles north, respectively. With a pontoon boat, you can see all three in a couple of hours. With a canoe or kayak, it's feasible to paddle to either Norton Falls or Hurricane Falls. Hurricane Falls can also be viewed roadside from Norton Road, which is south of the lake off NC 107.

While you're out, explore one of the islands or sunbathe on one of the natural sand beaches. Fishing is also popular. The lake is exceptionally clean because it is at the top of the watershed and fed by springs. At an elevation of 3,500 feet, this 1,462-acre lake creates 26 miles of shoreline.

Lake Glenville (Thorpe Reservoir) was formed when a dam was built on the West Fork of the Tuckasegee River. The project was in response to the power requirements of World War II. Each day, the plant generated enough electricity to produce aluminum for two B-17 Flying Fortress bombers. Power went on-line in October of 1941.

**DIRECTIONS:** **Leave Cashiers heading north towards Glenville on NC 107. Travel 5 miles to Signal Ridge Marina. Call ahead to reserve a boat. David and Jim practically live at the marina between Memorial Day and Labor Day. Call ahead for a reservations; the marina rents boats from March through the end of October.**

# SILVER RUN FALLS

[0.4 MILE ROUND-TRIP, EASY]

On our first visit to Silver Run Falls, our friend Alison Jones accompanied us. Writing is of her favorite hobbies, so we asked her if she'd like to write this section. Without hesitation, she agreed, and her help is much appreciated.

The trail to Silver Run Falls is almost completely level. Halfway to the falls, you must cross a small creek on a constructed footbridge. Just downstream, the small creek joins Silver Run Creek. These two creeks are part of the headwaters of the Whitewater River, where you'll find Whitewater Falls.

If you follow the sound of rushing water for several hundred yards, the trail will bring you out to a rock that is perfect for viewing this 25-foot falls. The blue-green water pours into a large, circular pool creating an inviting swimming hole. From the small sandy beach, two downed trees can be used to walk across the pool for a better photo angle. Silver Run Falls is surrounded by a damp forest of rhododendron, hemlock, and poplar.

**DIRECTIONS:** **Drive south from Cashiers on NC 107 for 3.5 miles where you will see trash dumpsters on the left. Travel another 0.5 mile to the second pulloff on the left after the dumpsters. The trailhead is at the utility pole, and the waterfall is in the Nantahala National Forest.**

# seventeen HIGHLANDS

**H**IGHLANDS IS AN ELEGANT mountain town. Main Street is lined with fashionable boutiques, fine restaurants, and exquisite specialty shops. Even the gas stations are attractive. It is difficult to find a chain store. A stroll around downtown Highlands is almost as much fun as a hike to one of the area's magnificent waterfalls.

Until 1981, when the community of Beech Mountain was incorporated, Highlands was considered the highest town east of the Mississippi. The average elevation is 4,118 feet. The Cherokee named this high land Onteeoorah, which translates loosely to "hill of sky."

The surrounding peaks range from 4,200 to 5,000 feet. The most famous, Whiteside Mountain, boasts sheets of granite ranging in height from 400 to 750 feet. From the summit at 5,000 feet, you can see for 50 miles in every direction.

Besides being one of the highest towns in the Blue Ridge, Highlands has almost as much rainfall as the western slopes of Oregon and Washington. The average annual rainfall is almost 80 inches. This abundant water feeds the headwaters of the Chattooga River and the Cullasaja River. There are also springs on almost every acre—nearly 200 within the town boundaries.

Add the altitude and rainfall to Highland's lack of polluting industry or agriculture, and the result is a special place, unique and diverse in its flora and fauna. From Wilson Gap Road, you can visit the second largest poplar tree in the East. To find out more about the area's plants and animals, go to the Highland's Nature Center on Horse Cove Road.

The Nature Center is open year-round. You can walk through the botanical gardens, listen to films and archaeological lectures, and let the kids attend educational classes. A group of citizens founded the Nature Center in 1927 to create a place for a display of plants, animals, minerals, and Indianartifacts. Over the years, hundreds of papers have been published based on the research performed here.

If you're lucky enough to be in the area in December when there's snow on the ground, head for Scaly Mountain, located 7 miles southwest of Highlands on NC 106. You can go snow tubing and then enjoy the Christmas parade put on by this small community of 300 people.

There is an interesting story behind the founding of Highlands. Legend tells of two land developers from Kansas, Samuel Truman Kelsey and Clinton Carter

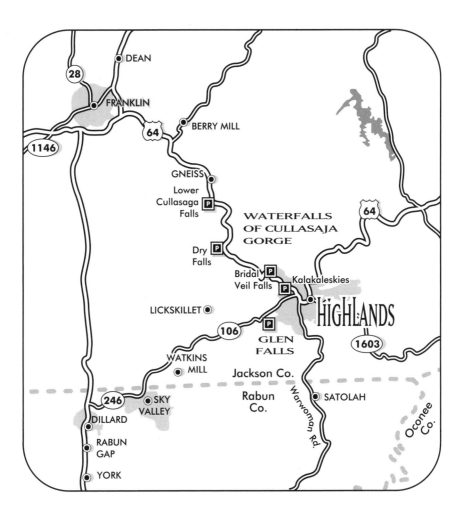

Hutchinson, who marked a spot on a map by drawing a line from Chicago to Savannah, and from New Orleans to Baltimore. They theorized that the intersection of these two lines would someday become a commercial mecca. The X marked the area of present-day Highlands.

Kelsey and Hutchinson purchased 839 acres from Captain J.W. Dobson of Horse Cove. The proposed settlement was established on March 30, 1875, but because the mountains were too steep for trains, and the mules were too slow, the initial dream of a great population center quickly faded. Yet the two men saw the magic in this place and set about promoting their new town.

As early as 1896, Kelsey and Hutchinson advertised Highlands as a health resort; the high altitude, a curative for many diseases like yellow fever, which plagued the low country of the Carolinas. Their brochures boasted unsurpassed beauty, along with few flies and no mosquitoes. The area's waterfalls were also used in promotion; publications told of the spectacular cascades of the Cullasaja River and other falls too numerous to mention.

Kelsey and Hutchinson didn't exaggerate. The cascades of the Cullasaja River are spectacular, and the area's waterfalls are too numerous to mention. Here are a few to get you started. Stop at the Highlands Visitor Center (open year-round on weekdays) in downtown to find out about other waterfalls in the area.

## GLEN FALLS

[ 2 MILES ROUND-TRIP, STRENUOUS ]

This is a three-for-the-price-of-one waterfall. It has three tiers, each about 60 feet high and viewed separately from different spur trails. However, the price is high because the trail is steep, descending almost 700 feet in a mile. The trip out is tough. The trail is a little rough in places, but it has wooden steps and signs marking some of the spur trails.

The falls, collectively known as Glen Falls, are located on the East Fork of Overflow Creek. Several spurs off the main trail give you a close-up look at the individual cascades. The first observation point, at the top of the first tier, is only ten minutes into the hike. From here, it looks like the falls are one huge drop. There are two other platforms beyond this point.

If 180 feet of falling water isn't enough, the Glen Falls Trail provides other splendid features. The vistas of the Blue Valley are exceptional. There are mature stands of pitch and white pine along the ridge above the falls, and vertical hillsides are covered with hardwoods and conifers. You will also find choice picnic sites near the beginning of the trail, but there are no picnic tables.

DIRECTIONS: **From Highlands, head west on US 64 to the junction of US 64 and NC 106. Go south on NC 106 for 1.7 miles and turn left at the sign for Glen Falls Scenic Area. This road is gravel and ends at a parking area after 1 mile. The trailhead is just beyond the information board. Be sure to take the trail to the left. (Chinquapin Mountain Trail is to the right.)**

*Glen Falls*

# WATERFALLS
# OF THE CULLASAJA GORGE

**KALAKALESKIES FALLS:** [No hike necessary]

**BRIDAL VEIL FALLS:** [No hike necessary]

**DRY FALLS:** [0.3 mile round-trip, Easy]

**LOWER CULLASAJA FALLS:** [No hike necessary]

The Cullasaja Gorge is a masterpiece. It would be difficult to find a more rugged river gorge anywhere in the Blue Ridge. The Cullasaja River runs parallel to US 64 between Highlands and Franklin. This stretch of road is a National Forest Scenic Byway. Considered one of the most beautiful routes in western North Carolina, this highway was carved into the side of a cliff.

In order to build the road, workers were repeatedly lowered from cliff tops in rope slings to drill holes and place dynamite. They blasted away solid granite. Construction began in 1928; and in 1929, an estimated 2,000 people attended a ceremony to unveil a monument to the founder of Highlands, Samuel Kelsey. The first gravel was unloaded in 1931, and the road was partially paved by 1932. It's a wonder the work was ever completed. Funds were denied by the federal government because of the extreme expense, and delays came from the road department because they were not enthusiastic about starting the hardest project of their careers.

Fortunately, the road was constructed, or most of us would never get to witness the Cullasaja River's unspoiled beauty and tremendous power. Stating that the river descends close to 2,000 feet in 7.5 miles should tell the story, but here's more. There are ripples and rapids, twist and turns, and many drops. These drops add up to several major falls and a dozen minor ones, each with its own unique personality.

Just below the dam on Lake Sequoyah at the upper end of the gorge, there is a series of small waterfalls collectively called the Kalakaleskies. Scramble down the bank to the river's edge and explore. This is the beginning of the many waterfalls on the Cullasaja River.

The dam was built in 1927 and measures 28 feet by 175 feet. It creates the 66-acre lake named after the famed Indian Chief, Sequoyah. This hunter and fur trader, who never attended school, developed a system of writing that enabled the Cherokees to read books and newspapers published in their own language. Sequoyah is the only Indian with a place in the Hall of Fame in Washington D.C.

The next waterfall comes with a legend. Indian maidens believed if they walked behind the falls in the spring, they would marry before the first snowfall. Thus, the name–Bridal Veil. Today, you can drive under the waterfall. Traffic was routed along the paved semicircle behind the falls before the construction of US 64. (Note: The Bridal Veil drive-thru is closed during the winter months due to ice on the pavement.)

Bridal Veil is a delicate falls, the water volume is small. The upper section clings to an 80-foot rock face and the lower section free falls about 40 feet. Bridal Veil Falls is incredible in the winter, when frozen spray adorns the plants, and icicles cling to the overhang. Because this waterfall is just 100 feet off the highway, it is the most well-known and photographed waterfall around Highlands.

Dry Falls boasts a very dry backside, which is where it gets its name, and its popularity. It is possible to walk under the falls without getting wet because a hollow area has been cut away by centuries of erosion. You can look out into the Cul-

*Lower Cullasaja Falls*

lasaja Gorge through the sheets of water. (*Note:* Be prepared to get soaked if the river is running high.

A set of steps and a paved walkway will take you to the viewing area. The river plunges 75 feet from a protruding shelf onto rocks just a few feet from the path. Rare plants, such as Rock Club Moss and Appalachian Filmy Fern, are watered by the constant spray. There is a sensational roar.

Don't turn back to Highlands until you've seen the last major waterfall in the gorge. It is a blockbuster. Lower Cullasaja Falls is higher and more captivating than any of the others. It crashes through the steep canyon over a series of wide ledges and then falls freely for 150 feet. The river splits into several dramatic cascades, each worthy of its own name. Dropping a total of 250 feet in 0.25 mile, Lower Cullasaja Falls is considered one of the most picturesque falls in North Carolina.

The best vantage point is from a paved shoulder off US 64. An unmaintained path (0.5 mile) will get you closer; but it is difficult, and downed trees obscure the falls. Fortunately, the view from the shoulder is stunning. This may not be a perfect place for a picnic, but your photograph is sure to be striking.

DIRECTIONS: **From Highlands, head west on US 64 towards Franklin. Within 2 miles you will be driving alongside Sequoyah Lake and then the dam will be visible on the left. Kalakaleskies covers a 0.25-mile stretch below the dam and there are several places to stop. Bridal Veil Falls is next on your right. There is a paved circular pulloff. Travel another 0.9 mile to the parking area for Dry Falls on your left. (There is a $2 fee for parking.) And finally, pull off on the shoulder after 5.5 miles to view Lower Cullasaja Falls. There is not a sign to mark the area, but you can't miss the falls. It is best to pass the falls, turn around, and come back to park.**

# LOWER SATULAH FALLS

*[No hike necessary]*

If you are traveling to Highlands from Walhalla, South Carolina, or if you are just interested in a pleasant drive, don't miss Satulah Falls. Also called Clear Creek Falls or Hidden Falls, it can be seen from an overlook on NC 28, just south of town. The creek lies along the boundary on the Nantahala National Forest.

Although the falls is about 0.25 mile away, you can hear the sound of rushing water from the overlook. I'd advise a fairly long lens in order to capture this 60-foot, sliding falls on film. But the photographic opportunities are not limited to the cascade; views of Rabun Bald and the Blue Valley are also possibilities.

After you leave the overlook and head back to Highlands, you will see the landmark cliffs on the south side of Satulah Mountain, a large rock outcropping with an elevation of 4,560 feet. In 1909, a few concerned citizens purchased 32 acres of this mountain with monies they raised. The land is an everlasting gift to the public.

# eighteen CHEROKEE

CHEROKEE IS MORE than a place, it is also a people. You may come to the town expecting to see tepees and painted warriors in feathered headdresses. And you will see those things—an illusion for the benefit of the tourist. The Cherokee inhabiting the Blue Ridge lived in structures made from wood, grass, and clay. There is more to this place and these people than tourist kitsch.

The Cherokee believed in a supreme being—the Creator—and they believed in an afterlife. The spirit, the very essence of the Cherokee Indian, is intrinsically tied to the Smoky Mountains. In fact, it is because of the mountains that the Cherokee Indian Reservation, known as the Qualla Boundary, exists today. The Cherokee, who refused to be forced from their homeland by the Removal Act of 1830, took harbor in the heart of the Sha-cona-ge, "the place of blue mist."

Long before white explorers came to the Blue Ridge, there were Indians here. Ethnologists generally believe that these natives began moving south nearly 1,000 years ago, settling in the Appalachians from the Ohio River south to northern Georgia and Alabama. The very birthplace of the Cherokee Indian was in the Smokies. Kituwha, the first Cherokee town, was located near Deep Creek Campground. The Cherokee believed that the Little People lived in the shadows of the mountains and kept the history of the tribe.

When the Spanish explorer Hernando de Soto encountered the Cherokee in 1540, he found a well-developed, unified, and gentle nation of approximately 25,000 people. They had an organized form of government and were the first of all the Indian tribes in North America to have a written form of language, invented by Sequoyah in the 1820s. Considered to be one of the most intelligent Indians in history, Sequoyah is the only person on record with the distinction of having designed an entire alphabet. It took him 12 years to create the system of symbols. Two years after he presented his alphabet to the Cherokee Council, *The Cherokee Phoenix* began circulation and nearly everyone who spoke Cherokee could read and write.

With exploration came the inevitable influx of settlers. Battles ensued over fur trade and land possession. During different periods of history, the Cherokee were both friend and foe to the white man. For example, they fought with the troops of General Andrew Jackson against the Creek Indians at the Battle of Horseshoe Bend

in 1814. This loyalty was not rewarded, however, as it was President Jackson who signed the act that forced the Indians westward.

The discovery of gold in the area sounded the final death knell for the Cherokee. Greedy settlers, not content to share the land, continued to force the Indians out. Continuing the tragic undertaking that Jackson had begun, President Martin Van Buren, in 1838, ordered General Winfield Scott to enforce the removal of all the Cherokee to land west of the Mississippi (now Oklahoma). About 18,000 Cherokee were rounded up and driven west over the Trail of Tears. An estimated one-fourth of the Indians died along the way from starvation, exposure, disease, and despair. One account from a government participant described it as "the cruelest work I ever knew."

About 1,000 Cherokee fled to the isolation of the mountains, mostly to the areas of Swain, Jackson, and Haywood counties of North Carolina. Tsali was one of these Cherokee refugees who was hiding his family. He had killed a soldier who mistreated his wife during the disastrous march west. Tsali's hiding place is believed to have been somewhere along what is now the Thomas Divide Trail in the Great Smoky Mountains National Park.

William Thomas, who as a white boy had been adopted by the Cherokee Chief Yonaguska, convinced Tsali to turn himself over to the U.S. government. The government agreed to pardon the remaining Indians hiding out in the mountains in exchange for Tsali's execution. Tsali gave himself up with the agreement that his sentence be carried out by his Cherokee brothers. Upon his death, the remaining Cherokee were allowed to return to their homeland. Although their land was much smaller and their numbers were greatly reduced, the Cherokee retained their mountain birthplace because of Tsali's sacrifice.

Later, as business chief of the Cherokee, Thomas was able to represent the Indians in land claims. He was a strong advocate in Congress for the rights of the Cherokee and had great influence on the establishment of the Qualla Boundary. In gratitude to Thomas, the Cherokee followed him into combat, fighting on the side of the Confederacy at the Battle of Deep Creek.

The 56,000-acre Qualla Boundary is located at the southern end of the Blue Ridge Parkway. The Great Smoky Mountains National Park forms the reservation's northern boundary. Covering parts of five North Carolina counties, the Qualla Boundary is home to the communities of Yellowhill, Birdtown, Painttown, Snowbird, Big Cove, and Wolftown. Government affairs are carried out by a 12-member tribal council, a principal chief, a vice-chief, and a number of tribal departments.

A visit to Cherokee, capital of the Eastern Band of the Cherokee Nation, offers numerous opportunities to learn about the Native Americans who first inhabited the mountains and valleys of the Great Smokies. The history, culture, and stories of the Cherokee people can be explored at the Museum of the Cherokee Indian, renovated in 1998 and located on US 441 at Drama Road. Visitors can watch audiovisual displays and view a priceless collection of artifacts.

Since 1950, *Unto These Hills,* a live drama, has vividly portrayed the saga of the Cherokee struggle. The play brings North Carolina history alive, from Hernando de Soto's arrival in 1540 through the removal of the Cherokee in 1839. The two-hour production is performed each summer in a beautiful outdoor theater.

*Little Creek Falls*

The Cherokee continue to preserve their culture through their traditional crafts. From mid-May through October, visitors can see Cherokee artisans at work at the Oconaluftee Indian Village, a re-created Cherokee village of the 1750s. Maintained by the Cherokee Historical Association, this full-size replica village has demonstrations of all the Cherokee arts such as canoe-making, pottery, beading, weaving, and chipping flint into arrowheads. Qualla Arts and Crafts Mutual offers many of these remarkable handcrafted wares for sale. It is recognized as the most outstanding Indian-owned and -operated crafts cooperative in the United States.

Cherokee is a town that owes its existence to the tourist industry. With that in mind, expect to find the usual trappings of tourism. Despite the crowds, summer traffic, and trinket shops lining the main road, it is easy to get back to nature. There is plenty of camping–24 campgrounds are listed on the town's website–and many of the sites are along the Oconaluftee River. The Cherokee KOA has more facilities than any campground in the Smokies.

For anglers, this is paradise. The Cherokee manage 30 miles of regularly stocked trout streams and six acres of ponds. More than two dozen local businesses offer one-day tribal fishing permits. Rent an inner tube for a ride on the Oconaluftee or Raven Fork rivers. Take a day trip into the Great Smoky Mountains National Park—just minutes away. The Cherokee Visitor Center in the center of town is the place to go for information on all there is to do in Cherokee.

As we hike the trails to the waterfalls in the Great Smoky Mountains National Park and on the Qualla Boundary, we felt the presence of Indians who must have used these same trails as footpaths. The spirit of the Cherokee people dwells in the forests and mountains. We wonder if the Indians were as captivated by the waterfalls as we are.

# LITTLE CREEK FALLS

[ 4 miles round-trip, Moderate ]

As with many things in life, there is a direct correlation between effort and reward. Little Creek Falls is no exception. You may be slightly winded or have tired legs from climbing the steep switchbacks by the time you get to the falls, but following this section of trail over streams and through dense rhododendron thickets is half the fun.

Little Creek cascades down hundreds of small sandstone shelves for a total height of 95 feet. The rock staircase magnifies the volume of the relatively small mountain stream as water dances from shelf to shelf. At the base of the falls, there is a small pool and a natural (but slippery) bridge formed by logs and assorted debris. Standing on the bridge, you can almost reach out and touch the falls. If you go 20–30 feet beyond the bridge, you'll get a more level perspective.

The trail crosses Little Creek three times, but some creative rock hopping will keep your feet dry. After the first stream crossing, where Little Creek runs into Cooper Creek, go another 100 yards and reach a fork. There are no trail markers, so be sure to go left. (Some kindhearted soul placed sticks on the ground in the shape of an arrow. We didn't notice them until after we had mistakenly taken the right fork, which leads you away from the falls.)

The trail becomes steeper as you climb Thomas Ridge for 1 mile. After two more creek crossings and several switchbacks, the sound of rushing water tells you the falls are just around the bend. From the far side of the pool at the base, the trail continues for 0.2 mile to the top of the falls.

DIRECTIONS: **From Cherokee, take US 19 south to its intersection with US 441. Continue 5.8 miles to the community of Ela. Turn right at the Cooper Creek General Store and follow Cooper Creek Road for 3.3 miles. (The pavement ends after 1.3 miles, and you need to bear right and stay along the creek.) You are looking for Cooper Creek Trout Farm. Please park at the gravel area across from the chain-link gate. No permission is necessary, but if you plan to stay overnight, check in with Doug Crockett. (The trout farm opens in March.) Begin by walking through the gate at the boundary for the Great Smoky Mountains National Park.**

# WATERFALLS ON PIGEON CREEK TRAIL

**MINGO FALLS:** [0.5 MILE ROUND-TRIP, MODERATE]

**UPPER MINGO:** [FALLS: 1 MILE ROUND-TRIP, STRENUOUS]

Literature for Great Smoky Mountains National Park describes Mingo Falls as a must-see for vacationers—even though it is not in the park! The reason? Mingo Falls is a most impressive sight. Although Mingo Falls is one of the highest waterfalls in the area, dropping 120 feet, this is not the only feature that sets it apart from other falls. The water seems to fall in slow motion. This surreal effect is created by the stratified sandstone ledges, hundreds of tiny stair-steps in the rock face that slow the water.

Upper Mingo Falls is not mentioned in the park's literature, however; and although there is a well-defined path, many people don't know about this hidden treasure. To unexpectedly discover Upper Mingo Falls is like finding money in an old jacket. Tucked away in a cove and shaded by rhododendrons, Upper Mingo Falls cascades 25 feet over beautiful, moss-covered rock.

Pigeon Creek Trail is within the Qualla Indian Reservation. The first several hundred yards are steep, then the trail levels off to the base of Mingo Falls. To reach the top of Mingo Falls and Upper Mingo Falls, take the left fork off the main trail before getting to the base of the falls, ascend two switchbacks, climb a hill, and continue straight ahead. When the trail forks again, go right for a glimpse of the middle cascade of Mingo Falls, or go left and climb the natural steps in a rock face to the top of Mingo Falls. The shaded trail to Upper Mingo Falls follows Mingo Creek back into the woods.

DIRECTIONS: From Cherokee, go north on US 441 to Big Cove Road. Follow it for 5 miles. Mingo Falls Campground is on the right, 1 mile past the Cherokee KOA. Mingo Falls Campground is tribal property and non-campground users are welcome to park in the designated area. Pigeon Creek Trail begins behind the campground water system.

# FLAT CREEK FALLS

[1.5 MILES ROUND-TRIP, MODERATE]

Most waterfall hikes culminate at the base of the falls where you can sit and watch the play of water. That's what we were expecting when we visited Flat Creek Falls, and we were a little disappointed to find that you can't see the falls from the trail. Hiking to Flat Creek Falls was like spending time and effort in unwrapping an elaborate package, only to find the box empty. The gift, though, was really the wrapping–the pleasure of the hike.

Rushing water serenades you as you follow Bunches Creek just east of Heintooga Bald in the Balsam Mountains. The northern harwood forest is a reminder of the high elevation, approximately 3,400 feet. At the highest point along the trail, you have a grand view of Balsam Mountain Ridge and the surrounding valley. You'll find an unusual hardwood tree after the second log bridge. It is huge and hollow–three of us fit into the cavernous trunk for a family photo.

When you near the top of the falls, a warning sign directs you right to a spur trail ending at the lip of the falls. It appears the trail continues to the left of the sign, but the abrupt drop and lack of view are good reasons to heed the suggestion to stop. Although Flat Creek disappears over the precipice, you have a great view of the creek looking upstream.

The best view of the falls is from Balsam Mountain Road, which runs along Heintooga Ridge near Wolf Laurel Gap. This is a good place to pull over and get out your binoculars. You will definitely need them because the waterfall is barely visible as Flat Creek plunges 200 feet down the distant mountain ridge. Flat Creek Falls is one of the highest waterfalls in the Great Smoky Mountains National Park.

DIRECTIONS: From Cherokee, head north on US 441 and pick up the Blue Ridge Parkway (turn right) before the entrance to Great Smoky Mountains National Park. Travel 11.1 miles and turn left onto Balsam Mountain Road. After 4.6 miles, pull over on the shoulder on the left for your best view of the falls. Then continue 0.8 mile to the trailhead on the left. (In the winter, be sure to check road conditions at the Oconaluftee Visitor Center, 0.8 mile up US 441 past the entrance to the Parkway.)

## SOCO FALLS

[ 0.1 MILE ROUND-TRIP, STRENUOUS ]

Soco Falls is a dichotomy, nature's splendor and man's trash. Unfortunately, the area around the pulloff and trail has become a convenient dumping ground. Take only memories, leave only footprints was never more applicable. Is Soco Falls worth a visit? Yes! And bring an empty trash bag. A trip here reminds us that the preservation of beauty is the responsibility of those who treasure it.

Soco Creek and a larger unnamed creek converge at right angles just south of Soco Gap to form an unusual 50-foot, double cascade called Soco Falls. As

*Soco Falls*

you face the falls, you'll notice Soco Creek entering from the left while the main cascade emerges from the shade, high above you. Leaping into full view, the water reflects the rays of the midday sun, creating a sparkling spectacle. The two creeks meet midway in their descent to the pool at the base of the falls. Soco Creek then flows into the Oconaluftee River.

From the trailhead, you can hear the falls. A steep descent brings you to an overlook that provides a good view. Going to the base of the falls is not recommended because it involves climbing down a near-vertical embankment.

Soco is derived from the Cherokee word Sogwo, meaning "one." Legend links the name to Hernando de Soto, the Spanish explorer. Supposedly, the Indians shouted "Soco" as they threw one of de Soto's soldiers over the falls to his death.

Soco Gap, the junction of US 19 and the Blue Ridge Parkway, marks the boundary of the Qualla Indian Reservation. This was the initial point of the 1876 U.S. survey that created the reservation. Soco Gap is also referred to as ambush place, where the Cherokees wiped out a raiding party of Iroquois Indians.

**DIRECTIONS: From Cherokee, travel about 10.5 miles north on US 19. There is a small pulloff, accommodating three or four cars, on the right side of the road. There are no signs, but the graffiti on the guardrail marks the spot. The trailhead is at the upper end of the guardrail.**

# nineteen BRYSON CITY

**B**RYSON CITY IS IN Swain County, where 86% of the land is owned by the federal government. Tourists are drawn here by the bountiful natural resources the county has to offer. They come for the mountains; 40% of the Great Smoky Mountains National Park is in Swain County and includes Clingman's Dome, the king of the mountains. They come for the water recreation; Swain County has four rivers–the Nantahala, the Tuckasegee, the Little Tennessee, and the Oconaluftee–and one lake, the beautiful Fontana Lake. And they come for the forests; part of the 517,436-acre Nantahala National Forest lies within Swain County. The county itself is small, with only about 60,000 acres, but more people visit Swain County than any other area of North Carolina.

The land that includes present-day Bryson City was first owned and inhabited by Cherokee Chief Big Bear. Under an 1817 treaty between the U.S. government and the Cherokee Indians, Chief Big Bear received 640 acres on the Tuckasegee River. This included the Indian village of Younaahqua (or Big Bear Springs) and the land west of the mouth of Deep Creek.

Chief Big Bear later sold a portion of his reserve to John B. Love, supposedly for two white horses and a rig. The land had several other owners over the years. One of these owners was Alfred Cline, whose widow, Lucy, donated 25 acres in 1873 for the town square of the county seat, which was then called Charleston.

Colonel Thaddeus Dillard Bryson bought a large tract of the land on the north side of the Tuckasegee River. He built a home and operated a gristmill at the mouth of Deep Creek. In 1889, the county seat was renamed Bryson City in honor of Thaddeus, who was the first to represent Swain County in the state legislature.

The Iron Horse came to Bryson City in 1884, and with it came a new way of life. Industry followed the railroad. The densely forested land and abundance of water made this prime timber property; logging became the backbone of the county's economy.

The railroad followed the Tuckasegee from the town of Sylva. The construction took a tremendous amount of manpower and convict labor was often used. During the building of the railway's Cowee Tunnel in December of 1883, a ferry carrying workers across the Tuckasegee capsized in the swift waters. Shackled together at the ankles, 19 men drowned and are buried in an unmarked grave on a nearby hillside. Their ghosts are said to haunt the tunnel.

In spite of the perils involved in its construction, the railroad proved to be a boon to Bryson City. It brought in tourists from the Lowlands and took freight to distant markets. The numerous logging operations depended on the railroad for their survival, and the mountain folk depended on the logging operations for a steady paycheck.

When the Great Smoky Mountains National Park was formed in the 1930s, logging ceased except on the county's private lands, and the railroad remained. In earlier times, the railroad was the only mode of transportation between communities; today the Great Smoky Mountains Railroad is a popular tourist attraction. The rail offers a number of round-trip excursions through this beautiful section of western North Carolina. The marvelous views of the Smokies and the nostalgic allure of the railroad combine to provide a magnificent trip.

The Nantahala Gorge Excursion begins at the Bryson City Depot, a 1900s railway station that has been restored, and takes you through the spectacular river gorge. The train crosses a 791-foot trestle over blue-green Fontana Lake, known as the Jewel of the Smokies. From a height of 179 feet, passengers can look down on the sparkling waters of Fontana. At 31 miles long, this is one of the largest lakes in the Appalachians. It was created in the 1940s when TVA built the massive Fontana Dam, which at 480 feet is the highest dam in the East.

Nantahala, the Cherokee word meaning "land of the noonday sun," aptly describes this deep and narrow gorge. The Nantahala River flows through the 8-mile gorge and lies in misty shadow except when the sun is directly overhead. Visitors watch and wave to the hundreds of folks in whitewater rafts, kayaks, and canoes. After witnessing their delight, you will want to add a rafting adventure to your list of fun things to do while in Bryson City. There are many companies to choose from. One outfitter, Wildwater Ltd., offers a ride on the railroad and a ride on the river for one price—the Raft & Rail.

The train stops at the Nantahala Outdoor Center (NOC), where passengers can spend some time before the return trip. In operation for over 30 years, NOC is one of the premier recreation outfitters in the world. In addition to raft trips and whitewater kayak and canoe instruction, NOC offers team building and mountain/road biking programs. The Adventure Travel Program schedules trips throughout the country and all over the world—in places such as Nepal, Costa Rica, New Zealand, Alaska, Mexico, and the Grand Canyon of the Colorado River.

Before the train departs, try Relia's Garden. This restaurant's delicious fare includes fresh ingredients from the gardens out front. Edible flowers accompany the beautifully prepared salads. The restaurant is run by Aurelia Kennedy who, along with her husband Payson, is one of the originals at NOC.

While it is wonderful to experience the splendor of this area from the comfort of a railway car, the only way to explore the magic of the mountains is to walk in them. The Great Smoky Mountains National Park is about 3 miles north of Bryson City, and Deep Creek Campground makes an excellent base for exploring the trails in the area. This developed campground has over 100 sites for tents or RVs, plus running (cold) water, flush toilets, and picnic areas. You can explore virgin forest and even arrange for the ranger to take you on a night walk.

This was Horace Kephart territory. The environmentalist, who was so instrumental in the park's formation, had a permanent camp called Bryson Place on

Deep Creek. He wrote of the area, "I lived for several years in the heart of it . . . always vital, growing new shapes of beauty from day to day."

The expropriation of Swain County for the Great Smoky Mountains National Park, Fontana Lake, and the Nantahala National Forest took away three-fourths of its taxable land, destroying the lumber industry and almost devastating the county financially. Ironically, the things that almost destroyed the county have become its greatest assets. The state's constitution contains an emphatic statement about protecting the land and water for the benefit of its citizens. Because the people of Swain County overcame temporary adversity for the long-term benefit of preservation, visitors follow hiking trails and mountain streams to the waterfalls around Bryson City. The website for the chamber of commerce, www.greatsmokies.com, has a page about waterfalls under Outdoor Adventure. The ones listed in this section are near the southern boundary of the Great Smoky Mountains National Park.

# JUNEYWHANK FALLS
[0.5 MILE ROUND-TRIP, EASY]

When you stand on the log bridge that crosses the middle of Juneywhank Falls, you are surrounded by the sights and sounds of rushing water. The 80-foot cascade begins above you, runs under your feet, and descends below you on its way to the valley floor to join Deep Creek. You have a spectacular view of the falls, as well as the forest with its abundant laurel, rhododendron, and holly.

The narrow bridge over Juneywhank Branch has handrails and is easy to traverse, but the look on the face of our terrified eight-year-old daughter, Cory, would not have confirmed this. "I'm not going across that bridge and you can't make me!" After some persistent encouragement, she succeeded and felt good about her accomplishment. Walking over a waterfall on a log bridge is quite an adventure for a kid and makes for good storytelling back at school.

Juneywhank Falls has an unusual name, probably for a local resident, Junaluska Whank. Called Juney by his friends, he was named after the famous Cherokee Chief Junaluska. Legend has it that Whank is buried close to the falls.

DIRECTIONS: **Leave Bryson City from the train depot, which is on the corner of Depot Street and Everett Street. Turn right (heading east) onto Depot Street and travel 4 miles to Deep Creek Campground. Depot Street will become West Deep Creek Road. You will find the main parking area 0.5 mile from the entrance. Walk** a couple of hundred yards back (along the road just traveled) to the trail marker on the right.

# WATERFALLS ON DEEP CREEK TRAIL

**TOMS BRANCH FALLS:** $\left[\text{0.4 MILE ROUND-TRIP, EASY}\right]$

**INDIAN CREEK FALLS:** $\left[\text{2 MILES ROUND-TRIP, EASY}\right]$

It would be hard to find a hike that offers more scenery and adventure than the Deep Creek Trail. You can walk along the creek and view two beautiful waterfalls and then ride the rollicking waters on an inner tube back to your car. During the summer, inner tubes can be rented at the campground entrance. Adventurous tubers put in 0.75 mile up the trail from the parking lot, while youngsters and first-timers start at the 0.5-mile mark. Repeat rides can provide a full day of entertainment. If you want to be a spectator, you can watch the fun from the footbridge over Deep Creek.

The trail parallels the creek as it follows a wide abandoned roadway with a mild slope. Kids won't notice the grade; however, at the end of a day of tubing, their parents might. You'll pass Toms Branch Falls on the right after 0.2 mile. For Indian Creek Falls, turn right onto Indian Creek Trail after about 0.8 mile, and reach the falls in a few hundred feet.

Toms Branch pours into Deep Creek over 80 feet of stratified sandstone forming a beautiful waterfall. These sparse but spirited waters shift left, right, and then left again as the cascade tumbles over seven multi-tiered ledges. Although the majority of hikers would not require a rest this early on the trail, there is a bench opposite the falls that provides an ideal spot to sit and ponder this delightful example of Mother Nature's handiwork.

Indian Creek Falls is a noisy and boisterous high-volume cascade that plunges 25 feet into a large inviting pool at the base. The main flow is on the left, with two smaller cascades on the right partially hidden by rhododendron and other vegetation. Another trailside bench provides a place to enjoy the sights and sounds of rushing water, and you can hike down the spur trail for a closer view.

DIRECTIONS: **Leave Bryson City and travel to Deep Creek Campground (see directions under Juneywhank Falls). The trailhead is at the upper end of the main parking lot.**

# twenty FRANKLIN

**F**RANKLIN, LOCATED in the mountains of western North Carolina on the banks of the Little Tennessee, has earned the title Gem Capitol of the World, and gem mining ranks alongside hiking to waterfalls as the primary draw for visitors. The area is a favorite spot for rock hounds, and you might be as lucky as one miner who found a 400+ carat ruby that was estimated to be worth $14,000.

You will find a large concentration of mines in the famous Cowee Valley, north of town, as well as others off NC 28 and US 441. Most gem mines are open from April through October and offer cutting and mounting, covered flumes, gift shops, picnicking, snack bars, and rest rooms. Visitors purchase native gemstone dirt and/or enchanted buckets (great for kids) for $5–15. By participating in this centuries-old tradition, you may find native garnets, amethysts, rubies, sapphires, and other semiprecious stones. For an introduction to the area's gems, minerals, and mining, visit the Gem and Mineral Museum housed in the old county jail. It opens annually in May (free admission) and will prove interesting to the rock hound and/or the history buff.

In addition to its rich natural resources, Franklin has an interesting history. Nikwasi (present-day Franklin) was once one of the largest villages in the Cherokee Nation. These Native Americans settled along the Little Tennessee and thrived in the eighteenth century. Nikwasi Mound, one of the best-preserved mounds in western North Carolina, is located on East Main Street. Man-made mounds were often the central point of a village and used for ceremonial rituals.

The Cherokee Indians began to give up their land in 1819 because of encroachment by white settlers, and pioneers flocked to the area with hopes of prosperity. The early pioneers were mostly Scotch-Irish, and the county developed quickly with the establishment of the nearby resort-town of Highlands (1875), the coming of the railroad, and the formation of the Nantahala National Forest. To learn more about the rich heritage of the area, visit the Macon County Historical Museum, which opened 1990. The museum is located inside a 1904 retail store, which was then the main fixture of town and is now of historical interest too.

There's more to Franklin than gem mining and visiting historic sites. Franklin has location and scenery. It is one of the few full-service communities along US 441 between Georgia and Great Smoky Mountains National Park. (Be sure to

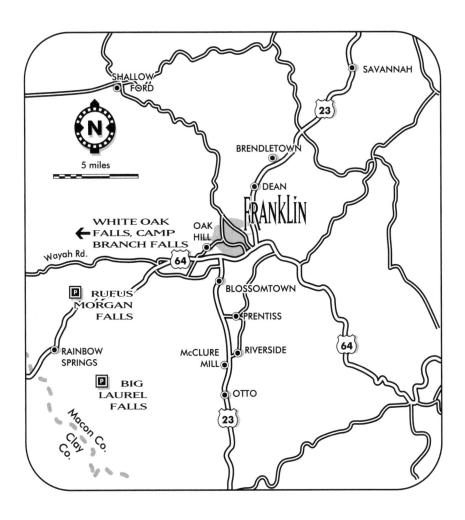

stop in the Smoky Mountains Welcome Center just south of town on US 441.) The town itself is surrounded by the 1.5-million-acre Nantahala National Forest, the largest of four national forests in North Carolina. And in fact, half of the county (Macon) lies in the national forest. Outdoor recreation abounds, and you can sight-see from one of many popular scenic drives. The office for the Wayah Ranger District is located 2 miles west of Franklin at Old US 64 and Sloan Road.

This town, with a permanent population of 3,300 people, doubles in number during the spring, summer, and fall, when vacationers arrive to enjoy the casual, small town atmosphere. Main Street is lined with antique shops, galleries, bookstores, and coffee shops. Most of the artisans that call Franklin home display their work through several co-ops. Don't miss the Uptown Gallery, a nonprofit, artist-run association.

On Saturday nights (at 7 p.m.) between June and October, Franklin hosts its famous Pickin' on the Square series. At the gazebo on the town square, you can enjoy free public concerts that feature bluegrass, country, and gospel–some of the best in the South. Be sure to bring a blanket or camp chair. For dinner before the show, try something from the gourmet menu at Frog and the Owl Kitchen on East Main Street. This restaurant serves international cuisine that is worthy of its wide acclaim. Also, Lucio's on Highlands Road features wonderful Italian dishes and great wines.

For a taste of the area's scenic drives, take Wayah Road (NC 1310), to the west of town. It is part of the 61-mile Mountain Waters Scenic Byway. This beautiful drive parallels Wayah (Cherokee for wolf) Creek and ascends Wayah Mountain on its way to Nantahala Lake, connecting with US 19 along the Nantahala River. Early in the trip, you can stop at Arrowood Glade Picnic Area, located on an old hatchery site, or later take the 4.5-mile side trip to Wayah Bald (5,342 feet), one of the tallest peaks in the area.

Forest Road 69 (gravel) leaves NC 1310 at Wayah Gap, and at mile 1.3, you will pass the Wilson Lick Ranger Station. Built around 1913, it was the first ranger station for the Nantahala National Forest. After another 3.2 miles, you'll reach a short trail that leads to a lookout tower (circa 1930) atop Wayah Bald and incredible views of the Southern Appalachains. Two famous trails cross the mountain here, the Appalachian Trail and the Bartram Trail.

As far as waterfalls go, your adventures will take you into the Nantahala National Forest and along the Nantahala River. The Wayah Ranger District is an area of mountains, valleys, lakes, rivers, wilderness, and old-growth forest. The 134,000 acres are part of the central section of the Nantalaha National Forest and include the remote Southern Nantahala Wilderness, the popular Standing Indian Area picnicking and camping grounds, and the Nantahala River, famous for whitewater rafting. The mountains rise to over 5,000 feet and include Standing Indian (elevation 5,499 feet), said to resemble a brave turned to stone. More than 50 miles of the Appalachian Trail follows the crest of the mountains to Wesser and is maintained by the Nantahala Hiking Club. Like panning for precious stones, hiking to the waterfalls in this area may reveal some wonderful treasures.

# WHITE OAK FALLS AND CAMP BRANCH FALLS

[No hike necessary]

There are two easy-access, roadside waterfalls in the Wayah District of Nantahala National Forest that are well worth visiting if you are on your way from Franklin to the Nantahahla River and Bryson City. The drive over to White Oak Falls and Camp Branch Falls is part of the Mountain Waters Scenic Byway (NC 1310).

White Oak Falls is a high-volume cascade that plummets over a rocky face, a freefall of 40 feet. Two hundred yards after the falls, White Oak Creek joins the Nantahala River. Although you can view the falls from your car, stretch your legs awhile and rock hop to the base of the falls or walk the paved road to see the falls from the top. Many of the local rafting-outfitter employees find the sun-drenched rocks are a perfect spot to read, eat lunch, or just while away the hours.

Sources at the Nantahala Outdoor Center verify that White Oak Falls has been run successfully by highly skilled kayakers. Despite the apparent absence of a clear route and the suicidal drop into a shallow rocky pool, there is a narrow line that can be negotiated if run perfectly. It looks impossible. We were told that the boaters who accomplished this feat were "true experts. . . if not slightly demented."

Camp Branch Falls is best viewed as you drive back down the mountain from White Oak Falls. Flowing through the Burning Town Area, Camp Branch Creek begins its descent from a mountain ridge as a narrow chute of water and quickly fans out. Dropping 150 feet over a series of ledges, Camp Branch Falls flows into the Nantahala River.

DIRECTIONS: **From Franklin, at the junction of US 64 and US 411, go west on US 64 for 3.7 miles and exit to the right at the brown sign marked "wayah bald." This is Old Murphy Road and you'll travel 0.2 mile to the Phillips 66 gas station. Take a left here on Wayah Road (NC 1310). Both falls are visible from the road en route to US 19 past Nantahala Lake (20+ miles).**

# BIG LAUREL FALLS

[1-MILE ROUND-TRIP, EASY]

Big Laurel Falls is especially popular with folks staying at the Standing Indian Campground in the Nantahala National Forest. The adjacent 10,900-acre

Southern Nantahala Wilderness includes Standing Indian Mountain (elevatioin 5,499 feet), named for resemblance to a Native American. And, the Appalachian Trail runs through the area.

The trail to the falls is primarily an old railroad grade. In the first 50 feet, the trail forks; bear right. Begin descending on switchbacks to Mooney Creek, which you cross on a bridge, before reaching another fork. A left leads to Timber Ridge Trail. Go right, following Mooney Creek, then up Laurel Creek to the waterfall. Big Laurel Falls drops in two tiers for a total of about 30 feet, and there is a small pool at the base. The creeks in this area form the headwaters of the Nantahala River, a popular whitewater run near Bryson City.

DIRECTIONS: **From Franklin, at the junction of US 64 and US 441, go west on US 64 for a little more than 9 miles and turn left onto Wallace Gap Road (Old US 64). Travel 1.5 miles and turn right onto Forest Service Road 67. (You will see a sign for Standing Indian Campground.) After 7 miles (5 miles past the Backcountry Information Center), reach a small pullout on the right.**

# RUFUS MORGAN FALLS

[1-MILE LOOP, MODERATE]

The Rufus Morgan Trail, a short loop, is cut out of a mountainside. You'll encounter some steps, narrow tread, and stream crossings. You'll pass through a mature hardwood stand before the waterfall and through an area where timber was harvested (until 1992) after the waterfall. Rough Fork Creek slides down a 70-foot drop into a small pool surrounded by ferns.

Follow the arrow at the trailhead, picking up the blue-blazed trail, and ascend up and to the right to encounter some switchbacks. You'll reach a small stream crossing at 0.2 mile and then intersect an old logging road. Continue straight ahead on the trail (not the wide dirt road) and descend. At 0.4 mile, cross Rough Fork Creek and walk upstream toward the small cascading waterfall. Veer left away from the stream to an 18-inch diameter Poplar tree with a blue blaze on it and take a sharp switchback-style right to ascend to the falls.

The waterfall and the trail are named for Albert Rufus Morgan, a naturalist and a minister who loved the mountains. Often called the one-man hiking club, he worked on trails in the area for 27 years, including the Appalachian Trail. He died in 1983 at the age of 97.

To finish the loop, retrace your steps to the 18-inch diameter Poplar, and instead of returning the way you came, turn right and mostly descend on switchbacks. At an unmarked, overgrown side trail, stay left and continue to follow the blue blazes down to a large, open grassy area, where you'll go left 0.1 mile to the forest road. Your car is parked 100 feet away on the left.

DIRECTIONS: From Franklin, at the junction of US 64 and US 441, go west on US 64 for 3.7 miles and exit to the right at the brown sign marked "wayah bald." This is Old Murphy Road and you'll travel 0.2 mile to the Phillips 66 gas station. Take a left here on Wayah Road (NC 1310) and continue 6.6 miles, passing Arrowhead Glade Picnic Area at 3.3 miles. Turn left onto Forest Road 388 (marked by a small brown sign). After 2 miles, look for a small pullout on the right and a brown sign indicating A. Rufus Morgan Trail. Note that FS 388 is closed in the winter.

*Rufus Morgan Falls*

# APPENDICES AND INDEX

SECTION *four*

# IMPORTANT ADDRESSES

**Alleghany Highlands Chamber of Commerce**
241 West Main Street
Covington, VA 24426
(540) 962-2178
members.aol.com/ahchamber

**Asheville Area Chamber of Commerce**
P.O. Box 1010
Asheville, NC 28802
(828) 258-6101
www.exploreasheville.com

**Blowing Rock Chamber of Commerce**
P.O. Box 406
Blowing Rock, NC 28605
(828) 295-7851; (800) 2950-7851
www.blowingrock.com

**Blue Ridge Parkway**
199 Hemphill Knob Road
Asheville, NC 28803
www.nps.gov/blri
(828) 271-4779

**Brevard/Transylvania Chamber of Commerce**
35 West Main Street
Brevard, NC 28712
(828) 883-3700; (800) 648-4523

**Bryson City/Swain County Chamber of Commerce**
P.O. Box 509
Bryson City, NC 28713
(800) 585-4497
www.greatsmokies.com

**Caesar's Head State Park**
8155 Geer Highway
Cleveland, SC 29635
(864) 836-6115
www.southcarolinaparks.com

**Cashiers Chamber of Commerce**
Box 238
Cashiers, NC 28717
(828) 743-5941
www.cashiers-nc.com

**Cherokee Welcome Center**
P.O. Box 460
Cherokee, NC 28719
(828) 497-9195; (800) 438-1601
www.cherokee-nc.com

**Chimney Rock Park**
P.O. Box 39
Chimney Rock, NC 28720
(800) 277-9611
www.chimneyrockpark.com

**Douthat State Park**
Route 1, Box 212
Millboro, VA 24460
(540) 862-8100

**DuPont State Forest**
P.O. Box 300
Cedar Mountain, NC 28718-0300
(828) 251-6509
www.dupontforest.com

**George Washington and Jefferson National Forest**
Glenwood-Pedlar Ranger District

P.O. Box 10
Natural Bridge Station, VA 24579
(540) 291-2188
www.southernregion.fs.fed.us/gwj

### Glasgow/Rockbridge County Chamber of Commerce

100 East Washington Street
Lexington, VA 24450
(540) 463-5375
www.lexrockchamber.com

### Gorges State Park

P.O. Box 100
Sapphire, NC 28774-0100
(828) 966-9099
www.ils.unc.edu/parkproject/visit/gorg/home.html

### Great Smoky Mountains National Park

107 Park Headquarters Road
Gatlinburg, TN 37738
(865) 436-1200
www.nps.gov/grsm

### Hanging Rock State Park

P.O. Box 278
Danbury, NC 27016
(336) 593-8480
www.ils.unc.edu/parkproject/visit/haro/home.html

### Highlands Visitor Center

P.O. Box 404
Highlands, NC 28741
(828) 526-2112
www.highlands-chamber.com

### Jefferson National Forest

New Castle Ranger District
Box 256
New Castle, VA 24127
(540) (864) 5195

### Linville/Avery County Chamber of Commerce

P.O. Box 335
Newland, NC 28604
(828) 898-5605; (800) 972-2183
www.banner-elk.com

### LittleSwitzerland/McDowell County Chamber of Commerce

1107 West Tate Street
Marion, NC 28752
(828) 652-4240
www.mcdowellnc.org

### Luray-Page County Chamber of Commerce

46 East Main Street
Luray, VA 22835
(540) 743-3915; 888-743-3915
luraypage.com

### Marion/McDowell County Chamber of Commerce

1170 West Tate Street
Marion, NC 28752
(828) 652-4240
www.mcdowellnc.org

### Mt. Mitchell State Park

2388 State Highway 128
Burnsville, NC 28714
(828) 675-4611
www.ils.unc.edu/parkproject/visit/momi/home.html

## Nantahala National Forest
Highlands Ranger District
2010 Flat Mountain Road
Highlands, NM 28741
(828) 526-3765
www.cs.unca.edu/nfsnc

## Nantahala National Forest
Wayah Ranger District
90 Sloan Road
Franklin, NC 28734
(828) 524-6441
www.cs.unca.edu/nfsnc

## Natural Bridge of Virginia
P.O. Box 57
Natural Bridge, VA 24578
(800) 533-1410

## Pisgah National Forest
Grandfather Ranger District
Route 1, Box 11-A
Nebo, NC 28761
(828) 652-2144
www.cs.unca.edu/nfsnc

## Pisgah National Forest
Pisgah Ranger District
1001 Pisgah Highway
Pisgah Forest, NC 28768
(828) 877-3265
www.cs.unca.edu/nfsnc

## Pisgah National Forest
Toecane Ranger District
P.O. Box 128
Burnsville, NC 28714
(828) 682-6146
www.cs.unca.edu/nfsnc

## Shenandoah National Park
3655 US 211 East
Luray, VA 22835
(540) 999-3500
www.nps.gov/shen

## Signal Ridge Marina
P.O. Box 489
Glenville, NC 28736
(828) 743-2143
www.signalridgemarina.com

## South Mountains State Park
3001 South Mountain Park Avenue
Connelly Springs, NC 28612
(828) 433-4772
www.ils.unc.edu/parkproject/visit/
somo/home.html

## Stone Mountain State Park
3042 Frank Parkway
Roaring Gap, NC 28668
(336) 957-8185
www.ils.unc.edu/parkproject/visit/stmo/
home.html

## There is More Ministries
Living Waters
Balsam Grove, NC 28708
(828) 884-6350

## Waynesboro/Greater Augusta Regional Chamber of Commerce
732 Tinkling Spring Road
Fisherville, VA 22939
(540) 949-8203
www.augustachamber.org

# BIBLIOGRAPHY

Adams, Kevin. *Waterfalls of Virginia and West Virginia*. Birmingham, AL: Menasha Ridge Press, 2002.

Adkins, Leonard M. *Walking the Blue Ridge*. Chapel Hill, NC: The University of North Carolina Press, 1991.

Albright, Rodney and Priscilla. *Walks in the Great Smokies*. Chester, CT: Globe Pequot Press, 1990.

Biggs Jr., Walter C. and James F. Parnell. *State Parks of North Carolina*. Winston-Salem, NC: John F. Blair, Publisher, 1989.

Boyd, Brian. *Waterfalls of the Southern Appalachians*. Conyers, GA: Ferncreek Press, 1990.

Bryson City Genealogical and Historical Society. *100 Years of Progress*. Bryson City, NC: Chamber of Commerce, 1989.

Cantu, Rita. *Great Smoky Mountains: The Story Behind the Scenery*. Las Vegas, NV: KC Publications, 1979.

Catlin, David T. *A Naturalist's Blue Ridge Parkway*. Knoxville, TN: University of Tennessee Press, 1984.

Colbert, Judy and Ed. *Virginia: Off the Beaten Path*. Chester, CT:   Globe Pequot Press, 1986, 1989.

Corey, Jane. *Exploring the Waterfalls of North Carolina*. Chapel Hill, NC: The Provincial Press, 1991.

Crandall, Hugh. *Shenandoah: The Story Behind the Scenery*. Las Vegas, NV: KC Publications, 1990.

de Hart, Allen. *North Carolina Hiking Trails*. Boston, MA: Appalachian Mountain Club Books, 1988.

Frome, Michael. *Strangers in High Places*. New York, NY: Double-day and Company, 1966.

Hampton, Bruce, and David Cole. *Soft Paths*. Harrisburg, PA: Stackpole Books, 1988.

Hanson, Peggy, and Frances Pledger. *Touring Transylvania*. Brevard, NC: Highland Publishing, 1986.

Hubbs, Hal, Charles Maynard, and David Morris. *Waterfalls and Cascades of the Great Smoky Mountains*. Seymour, TN: Panther Press, 1992.

Jolley, Harley E. *The Blue Ridge Parkway*. Knoxville, TN: University of Tennessee Press, 1969.

Johnson, Randy. *The Hiker's Guide to Virginia*. Helena and Billings, MT: Falcon Press, 1992.

Logue, Victoria, Frank Logue, and Nicole Blouin. *Guide to the Blue Ridge Parkway*. Birmingham, AL: Menasha Ridge Press, 1997.

McIntosh, Gert. *Highlands, North Carolina. A Walk into the Past*. Highlands, NC: Published by the author, 1983.

Morrison, Mark. *Waterfalls Walks and Drives of Northeast Georgia and the Western Carolinas*. Douglasville, GA: H.F. Publishing, 1992.

Pitzer, Sara. *North Carolina: Off the Beaten Path*. Chester, CT: Globe Pequot Press, 1990.

Plemmons, Jan C. *Treasures of Toxaway*. Jacksonville, FL: By the author, 1984.

Potomac Appalachian Trail Club. *Appalachian Trail Guide to Shenandoah National Park*. Vienna, VA: By the author, 1986.

Roe, Charles E. *North Carolina Wildlife Viewing Guide*. Helena and Billings, MT: Falcon Press Publishing Company, 1992.

Shoemaker, Michael T. *Hiking Guide to the Pedlar District: George Washington National Forest*. Washington, DC: Potomac Appalachian Trail Club, 1990.

Tinsley, Jim Bob. *The Land of the Waterfalls: Transylvania County, North Carolina*. Brevard, NC: J.B. Tinsley and Dottie Tinsley, 1988.

Valentine, James. *North Carolina*. Portland, OR: Graphic Arts Center, 1990.

Wenberg, Donald C. Blue *Ridge Mountain Pleasures*. Chester, CT: Globe Pequot Press, 1988.

# INDEX